Life of Margaret Beaufort, Countess of Richmond and Derby

Caroline Amelia Halsted, Margaret Beaufort

BIBLIOLIFE

LIFE

OF

MARGARET BEAUFORT,

COUNTESS OF RICHMOND AND DERBY,

Mother of King Henry the Seventh.

BY

CAROLINE A. HALSTED.

"The famous Margaret, Countess of Richmond, whose merit exceeds the highest commendation that can be given; and from whom the royal family of England is descended." CAMDEN.

LONDON:
SMITH, ELDER AND CO. CORNHILL.

1839.

THIS MEMOIR

OBTAINED THE HONORARY PREMIUM

AWARDED BY

THE DIRECTORS OF THE GRESHAM COMMEMORATION,

MDCCCXXXIX.

EDWARD EARL OF DERBY,

BARON STANLEY,

OF BICKERSTAFFE, IN THE COUNTY OF LANCASTER,

KNIGHT OF THE MOST NOBLE ORDER OF THE GARTER.

MY LORD,

IT is with feelings of extreme satisfaction that I do myself the honor of dedicating to your Lordship the following Memoir of the illustrious consort of your great progenitor, Sir Thomas Stanley, first Earl of Derby.

Under no patronage could the life of MARGARET BEAUFORT appear with so much propriety as that of her lineal descendant, and the present representative of the noble personage, who on the field of Bosworth placed the Crown

upon the head of his royal son-in-law, King
Henry the Seventh, who first hailed him as
Monarch of England, and who received from
his hands that Title which, during the long period
of three centuries, has ever been "spotless and
free from stain."

With the ancient dignities, and vast possessions
of your illustrious house, your Lordship has in-
herited the eminent virtues, steadfast loyalty, and
lofty patriotism of your ancestors; to which,
permit me to add, are united a grace and kindness peculiarly your own.

I have the honour to remain,

My Lord,

Your Lordship's

Obliged, and most obedient Servant,

CAROLINE A. HALSTED.

Newlan House, Lymington,
   29th March, 1839.

PREFACE.

THE Crown of England after a lapse of glorious years again encircles the brow of a female Sovereign. Though few Queens have swayed the sceptre of these realms, they have all been descended from MARGARET BEAUFORT, the eminent lady whose eventful career is recorded in the following pages.

As the progenitrix of the present Royal family of England, her name alone would attract attention, even were it not connected with the pedigree on which King Henry the Seventh founded his chief pretension to the Throne.

But, the Countess of Richmond has higher claims to respect than any arising from mere hereditary distinctions. It is her goodness, and the benefits which she has conferred upon her country by her encouragement of literature and her munificent endowments, that constitute the charm which for centuries has rendered the "Venerable Margaret" an object of gratitude and admiration. It is her Christian character, her moral virtues, her high integrity during that dark period when temptations to disloyalty and ambition assailed the collateral branches of Royalty to a degree scarcely comprehensible in the present age, that has secured for this illustrious Princess so exalted a position among the most dignified females of England.

It is hardly credible that a paucity of material should have kept in shade so distinguished a person as the "Lady Margaret," or that little should be known of her, besides the brief, though enthusiastic, notices which commemorate her name. Unhappily, however, no portion of the national records is so defective and confused as those relating to the reigns of Henry the Sixth, Edward the Fourth, and Richard the Third.

The art of printing by which knowledge has been so wonderfully diffused, tended nevertheless at its introduction, to retard the authentic detail of passing events. Its astonishing powers by superseding the use of manuscripts, deterred the professional copyists from continuing a task thus wrested from them by a powerful and irresistible competitor ; while the early printers multiplied copies of such proceedings as had been committed to writing, and neglected more recent transactions as less interesting to their readers, and less lucrative to themselves, than the philosophical or legendary lore of the olden time. This fact, and the unsettled state of the kingdom during the civil wars of York and Lancaster, the destruction of family archives by the attainder, and execution of so many of the nobility and gentry, the danger of expressing opinions on political affairs, or promulgating anecdotes of persons allied to Royalty, sufficiently explain the cause of the acknowledged and lamentable imperfection in all materials for the history and biography of that period.

These difficulties have been sensibly felt in collecting facts for the Memoir now offered to the public ; yet the interest that attaches to the Lady Margaret, as the first female in England, who made intellectual attainments at once the pursuit and ornament of life ; and the beautiful eulogiums which were considered due to her by contemporary writers, when briefly but glowingly recounting her deeds of charity, and her patronage of learning, has lightened the author's toil, and left but one feeling predominant, that of regret, that the task of delineating so admirable a person had not fallen into abler hands.

The merit, however, of selecting the Life of Margaret Beaufort, and its consequent publication, belongs to a society whose efforts to advance historical knowledge, and whose exertions to rescue from oblivion characters and events hitherto concealed, deserves, as it indeed receives, the thanks of the literary world.

No subject perhaps could have been more appropriately chosen than the history of the parent of King Henry the Seventh, for the prize which was to be awarded at the auspicious commencement of the reign of our present gracious Sovereign ; to whom the females of Britain look with duty and affection,—with pride as women, with devotion as subjects.   As the successful competitor, the Author was called upon to publish the Essay to which the premium had been adjudged; and it then became her anxious desire to render the work as complete as so interesting a subject deserved.

To effect this, information has been sought

from many private and unpublished sources, and the original of such documents as were accessible have been diligently consulted. No available contemporary statement has been neglected — the Harleian, Cottonian, and Lansdowne MSS. have been attentively examined, and reference made to the archives of those collegiate establishments which owe so much to their eminent Foundress.

To Sir Harris Nicolas, the Author feels especially bound to express her sense of his readiness to afford every information in his power; and to acknowledge with gratitude that courtesy which so materially enhanced his kindness.

Under all the circumstances above stated, she cherishes the hope that indulgence will be extended to her as the medium of making more generally known a character so noble in every relative duty of life, as that of MARGARET, COUNTESS OF RICHMOND AND DERBY, who has been justly styled "the brightest ornament of her sex in the fifteenth century."

THE LIFE

OF

MARGARET BEAUFORT.

It has been justly observed, that the simple
mention of a great name often conveys a
higher degree of praise than the most laboured
panegyric or diffuse encomium. In few instances
has the truth of this assertion been more strongly
verified than in the subject of the present memoir.
The students of Christ's and of St. John's Colleges, Cambridge, can testify to the enthusiasm
with which strangers greet the statue of their
eminent foundress, by the simple exclamation of
—" There is the venerable Margaret."[1]

At the sister University, her titles—her greatness—her munificence—her piety—all seem em-

[1] " Foremost, and leaning from her golden cloud,
  The venerable Margaret see." GRAY.

bodied by common consent in the all-sufficient designation of " The Lady Margaret." No expletive is requisite, no further definition is required; and the descendant of princes—the mother of kings—she who was destined to wreathe with the peaceful olive the blood-stained rose of Lancaster, and the withered rose of York, is better known by the unpretending appellation of ' MARGA- RET BEAUFORT,' than by the high-sounding epi- thets of titled dignity which graced the styles of the parent of King Henry the Seventh,—who was her- self by descent, a Lancaster—by birth, a Somerset —by marriage, a Tudor, a Stafford, and a Stanley.

It may appear somewhat remarkable that an individual so elevated in rank, so noble in action, so illustrious in the opinion of her own and of suc- ceeding ages, should have remained thus long without a more detailed and minute account of her important life and proceedings. Rather, however, on reflection will it seem matter of aston- ishment, that without a contemporary biographer, her fame should have outlived the turbulent period in which she flourished, and her memory have sur- vived undiminished in estimation and uninjured by time, which so often obliterates exemplary deeds, while it only casts a veil over those that are evil.

Margaret of Lancaster was born before the art of printing had enabled the admirers of the great and good to perpetuate their noble acts; and she pursued her bright and glorious career, with so much humility during England's darkest era, that the mild light which her virtues shed upon the land of her birth, rather tended to illuminate the path of others than to enlighten her own. It was on the public receptacles of learning, piety, and knowledge, that it shone with resplendent lustre, —those noble institutions that were to benefit ages then in futurity, and which her liberality founded, endowed, and perpetuated.

Not a single collected account appears to be extant of this distinguished lady; but the annals of her time are so replete with brief memorials of her charitable and munificent actions, that like the tributary streams which, from minute sources, gradually swell the wide expanse of a mighty river, so amongst the archives of her colleges, and from the scholastic manuscripts and rare notices of the far-distant and unlettered age in which she lived, a mass of facts may be elicited, which, linked together in chronological order, forms a faithful and attractive portraiture of that noble mind, whose vicissitudes, trials, and genuine goodness, rendered her alike deserving of the respect of her contemporaries and the admiration of posterity.

Though deriving by comparison less celebrity from her high birth and exalted rank, than from that singular rectitude of heart and purpose, which under peculiarly trying circumstances marked her progress from childhood to old age ; yet, as the troubles which invigorated her mind arose in great measure out of her descent from the blood royal of England, it becomes essential to a true interpretation of many facts interwoven with her singular history, briefly to trace her parentage ; and before entering upon her private and personal memoirs, to go back a few years, and sketch the nature of that illustrious connection with the family of Edward the Third which at times rendered her an object of envy and suspicion—too often of persecution and oppression—to that branch of the Plantagenets which held the sceptre of England during the prime of her days.

John of Gaunt (" time honoured Lancaster") was the fourth son of King Edward the Third, born in 1340, and surnamed of Gaunt, or Ghent, from his mother Philippa of Hainault, having given him birth in that city. He was the active coadjutor, with his gallant brother the Black Prince, in most of the valorous actions which shed such lustre on the chivalric period in which they flourished.[1]

At the age of nineteen, he married his cousin Blanch, younger daughter and eventually sole heiress of Henry Duke of Lancaster, surnamed the Good ; who brought to him the duchy,[2] and in whose right he assumed the title, which was

[1] Baker's Chron. p. 132.   [2] Anglorum Speculum, p. 967.

confirmed to him by his father Edward the Third, in the year 1362.

By this marriage, John of Gaunt became the most extensive landholder in England, having estates in eighteen English counties, besides lands and castles on the Continent, and property of great value in the principality of Wales. The alliance was nevertheless one of pure affection. Blanch of Lancaster was his near kinswoman, and the "ladye love" of his boyhood. Their romantic courtship has been immortalized by Chaucer in his allegorical poem of the "Parliament of Birds,"[1] and their happiness in the nuptial state is commemorated by the same poet, in his "Book of the Duchess,"[2] written on occasion of the death of this amiable princess, at the early age of twenty-eight, about ten years after her marriage. The result of their union was two daughters, and an only son, afterwards King Henry the Fourth, surnamed of Bolingbroke, from a castle of that name appertaining to his mother in Lincolnshire, where he was born,[3] but more generally known by the title of Earl of Hereford, which he assumed in right of his wife, who was the daughter and co-heiress of Humphry de Bohun, whose honours and estates devolved on his daughters at his decease. By his means

---

[1] Godwin's Chaucer, vol. ii. p. 223.   [2] Verse 414.
[3] Verse 1279.

the crown of England first came to the house of Lancaster, and through his inheritance from that powerful family, the greatest patrimony of any subject prince in Christendom became annexed to the regal possessions, the peculiar immunities, privileges, immense wealth, and power of the Duchy of Lancaster, having been considerably extended by John of Gaunt's influence over his father, Edward the Third.

On the death of the Lady Blanch, and about two years after that event, the Duke espoused Doña Constantia, daughter and co-heiress of Peter the Cruel, King of Castile and Leon,[1] whom, in conjunction with his brother Edward the Black Prince, he had reinstated in his kingdom a few years previously.

On the death of this monarch, his two daughters fled from the persecutions of an uncle, who had usurped their father's crown, and took refuge in Gascony, where John of Gaunt resided at the time of his widowhood, and where, in 1372, he was united to the eldest of these princesses, whose cause he asserted by force of arms, and in whose right he adopted the title of the deceased king. The issue of this marriage, was an only child, a daughter, who espousing the Prince of Asturias, eldest son of the King of Spain, regained, on his accession to the throne, her grandfather's posses-

---

[1] Testamenta Vetusta, vol. i. p. 140.

sions ;[1] the Duke of Lancaster having surrendered
the claims of Doña Constantia, and his own
assumed title, to the youthful pair, on the consideration of a suitable pension for life to himself and
his consort. The descendants of this daughter by
his second marriage, continued kings of Spain
until the year 1700 ; and her eldest sister by the
Lady Blanch, of Lancaster, being united about
the same period to John King of Portugal, her
posterity for seven generations governed that
kingdom, and continued to do so until it was
united to Spain in the year 1640. Thus were
the children of this heroic prince seated at the
same time on the thrones of England, Spain, and
Portugal.

It has been already observed, that by his two
marriages, John of Gaunt had only one son; but,
by her who eventually became his third wife, he
had three others born out of wedlock, who are
usually characterized by the appellation of " his
valorous offspring."[2] Their influence in after
years, both in Church and State, would alone
have immortalized their names, had not the fatal
quarrel of the Rival Roses, begun by the usurpation of his legitimate son Henry the Fourth, been
destined to be healed by the descendants of the
eldest of these his illegitimate children, in the

[1] Sandford's Genealogy.   [2] Baker's Chron. p. 141.

person of Henry the Seventh, the son of Margaret of Lancaster.

The constant intercourse with France, and the numerous alliances which political expediency produced in the higher ranks of society, caused, as a natural result, an extensive connection amongst the intermediate classes also ; and consequently many foreigners were attached to the persons or household of our most distinguished nobles.   On the marriage of John of Gaunt with the Princess Blanch of Lancaster, Katherine, the beautiful and accomplished daughter of Sir Payne de Roet, a native of Hainault, and king-of-arms of the province of Guienne, was engaged to attend on the person of the young duchess.[1]   Her sister was " *domicella,*" or, as it is termed, maid of honour to Philippa, Queen of Edward the Third, an appointment which is now reserved exclusively for ladies of honourable birth.[2]

Both sisters were highly accomplished, the French having cultivated the elegancies of life at a much earlier period than their neighbours; and Katherine became so high in favour with the Princess Blanch, that she enjoyed her peculiar confidence, and was entrusted with the care and superintendence of her cherished offspring. During their early infancy, however, the beautiful Gas-

[1] Sandford's Genealogy, p. 253.
[2] Godwin's Life of Chaucer, vol. ii. p. 198.

coyne married Sir Otes Swynford, of Ketelthorpe, in Lincolnshire; but she does not appear to have been wholly separated from her illustrious patrons; for, about the time of their union, it is recorded that her husband was a knight in the retinue of the Duke of Lancaster, and as such, received letters of protection when with him in Gascony. 40 Ed. 3, 1366.[1]

On the death of the Princess Blanch, Lady Swynford was solicited by John of Gaunt to take the entire charge of his bereaved children; and the frequent visits of the prince to the nursery is said to have laid the foundation of that attachment, which formed so marked a feature in the after life of this distinguished warrior.[2]

Within a year of the marriage of John of Gaunt with Constance of Castile, the still lovely and fascinating Gascoyne became a widow, and after a brief interval she was once more permanently attached to the household of the noble duke, being engaged in the capacity of governess to his daughters.

The union of John of Gaunt with the Princess of Castile was not, like that with the Lady Blanch, one of affection; but on the contrary, a match exclusively of ambition.

Doña Constantia was amiable, gentle, and vir-

tuous to a high degree ;[1] but the affections of
her princely partner were fixed on another, and
Katherine Swynford, with the laxity of morals
common in that period, and especially in the South,
the land of her birth, became the mistress of her
noble employer, though ostensibly the instructress
of his children.

Among the vast possessions which accrued to
the Duke of Lancaster, in right of his first wife
the Lady Blanch, was the castle and town of
Beaufort, in Anjou.[2] In this castle, and during
the life-time of the Princess Constance, Katherine
Swynford in the course of time gave birth to four
children ; viz., John, afterwards created Earl of
Somerset ; Henry, the imperious Cardinal Beaufort ; Thomas, the valiant Duke of Exeter; and
Joan, grandmother (by marriage with Sir Ralph
Nevill, first Earl of Westmoreland) of King
Edward the Fourth and Richard the Third, as
also of the renowned Earl of Warwick, whose
powerful influence in a future reign gave alternate
ascendancy to the York and Lancastrian factions.

These children were all surnamed "De Beaufort,"[3] in consequence of their birth in that patrimonial castle of the Lancasters,[4] and from that

[1] Buck, Rich. III. p. 45.   [2] Collins' Peerage, vol. iv. p. 388.
[3] Excerpta Hist. 152.
[4] The Lordship and Castle of Beaufort, in Anjou, came to
the House of Lancaster with Blanch of Artois, Queen of
Navarre, wife of Edmund the first earl of Lancaster.

circumstance, they bore a portcullis for the cognizance of their family,[1] which device was frequently introduced among the elaborate ornaments which characterise the superb architectural buildings of the Tudor period.

On the death of his second wife Constance, to whom he was united for twenty-two years, John of Gaunt obtained the legitimation of his children by Katherine Swynford, first in a bull granted by Pope Urban the Sixth, then by a charter from his nephew Richard the Second,[2] and finally by act of parliament confirming and enlarging these indulgences. This important matter being effected, to the wonder of all men, and to the extreme annoyance of his kindred,[3] the prince towards the close of his eventful life, elevated their mother to the rank of a royal duchess; making her his third wife, on the 13th January, 1396; thus proving to the last the strong influence she had possessed over him for twenty years;[4] and this not merely by their union, but by the favour he lavished on her sister, who after the demise of Queen Philippa had espoused Chaucer, the poet laureate,[5] and to whom he is said to have allotted the rich demesnes and castle of Donnington in Suffolk, adding many other testimonies of

[1] Bakers' Chron. 132. [2] Rot. Parl. Ann. 20, Rich. II.
[3] Dugdale, Tome II. p. 119. [4] Excerpta Hist. p. 152.
[5] Godwin's Chaucer, vol. ii. p. 199.

good will to mark their consanguinity, after his marriage with Katherine Swynford. She survived her princely consort four years, and dying in 1403, was interred in Lincoln Minster, where her monument yet remains on the west side of the altar.

Attention must now be centered in the issue of this his third wife, it being irrelevant to trace the career of any other of John of Gaunt's numerous progeny, further than to observe, that Henry of Bolingbroke, his eldest and lawful son, having dethroned his cousin, the only child of Edward the Black Prince, about twelvemonths after the veteran chieftain's decease, forcibly took possession of the crown of England, by the title of Henry the Fourth, and throughout his reign was marked in kindness and affectionate treatment to his now acknowledged brothers the De Beauforts. They were joint inheritors with him of the immense possessions left by John of Gaunt; but as regards his usurpation of the throne, no rivalry could be apprehended; as although the act of parliament wiped off the stain of their birth, yet it was silent as regards all regal claims connected with the House of Lancaster. It neither elevated them to the rank of princes,[1] nor did it empower them to adopt the name of Plantagenet,[2]

[1] Buck's Rich. III. p. 45.

[2] In a brief notice, however, of Margaret Beaufort, in the Cotton. MSS. (Vitellius, C. xvii. f. 329.) the grandson of

which had been borne as the surname of their father's family by all the blood royal of England, since the time of their common ancestor Henry the Second.

John de Beaufort, the eldest son of Katherine Swynford, was created Earl of Somerset during the life-time of his father, with which dignity he was invested on the occasion of the above-named patent of legitimation being confirmed by the authority of Parliament, 29th Sept. 1397.[1] Recent discoveries have brought to light a remarkable fact, relative to the true purport of the act above cited ; but it will be sufficient at present merely to observe, that before his legitimation,[2] the arms of Sir John Beaufort were per pale argent and blue, (the colours of the livery of the House of Lancaster) having, on a bend, the arms of England, and surmounted by a label of those of France, which was latterly used by John of Gaunt ; but when Sir John Beaufort was raised to the dignity of Earl of Somerset, he discontinued the bearings which were assigned to him before his legitimation, and his seals contain the entire arms of the Prince his father : viz. France and England, quarterly, within a bordure, gobony, argent, and

John of Gaunt, and the son of the above named earl, is styled " The Lord John Plantagenet, Duke of Somerset."

[1] Excerpta Historica, p. 153.

[2] Willement's roll of arms, of the reign of Rich. II.

azure; thus proving that he considered himself entitled to the coat armour of his illustrious parent.

He left at his death, in 1410, four sons and two daughters. The king stood sponsor for his heir and successor Henry, who was baptized in 1401;[1] but the young earl dying in his minority, the title and possessions devolved on John, the second son, whose martial exploits are minutely recorded in the chronicles of the age in which he flourished.

The castle of Beaufort, in Anjou, appears to have continued the inheritance of these descendants of John of Gaunt; for this John, his grandson, when quite a youth, was taken prisoner while crossing the marches[2] that adjoined it, after a conflict between the French and Scots against the English, in the reign of Henry the Fifth; from which period began that brilliant career which has rendered his name so conspicuous in the warlike annals of the fifteenth century.

Recovering his freedom, the prime of his life was passed, with little intermission, in prosecuting those sanguinary wars with France which for years devastated that country, and impoverished our own; and in consideration of his valiant exploits, especially at the siege of Harfleur, he was advanced

[1] Baker's Northamptonshire, p. 55.
[2] Dugdale's Baronage, tome 2.

to the rank of Duke of Somerset and Earl of
Kendale, made Lieutenant of the Duchy of Aqui-
taine, and Captain-general of the whole realm of
France and Normandy.[1] Dissatisfied, however,
at the Duke of York being preferred to himself,
as regent of that kingdom, in 1436, he retired for
a brief period from active service, and returning
to England, became enamoured with Margaret,
the attractive widow of Sir Oliver St. John, only
daughter and heiress of John Lord Beauchamp,
of Powyke, whose wealth and high estate were
declared in the almost regal splendour she maintained at her manor of Bletshoe, in Bedfordshire.
He was married to her in the thirty-sixth year of
his age; and the issue of their union was one child,
a daughter, in whom were united the vast riches,
exalted rank, and noble qualifications, of a long
line of ancestry; a line whose heroic deeds might
well have kindled within her the spirit and courage
of a Joan of Arc, or the ambition of a Margaret
of Anjou. But the softer virtues cradled the
infant, to whom the martial exploits of her ancestors, and the troubled period of her birth seemed
to have promised a ruder nurture. Religion
breathed complacently on the descendant of the
valiant chieftain who supported the cause of
Wickliffe and openly espoused the tenets of the
father of the Reformation. The genius of litera-

[1] Baker's Chron. p. 185.

ture hovered round the great grand-daughter of the friend of Chaucer—the patron of Lydgate— and the moral Gower; while Peace, Charity, and Love, watched over the offspring of the exemplary Queens Eleanor of Castile and Philippa of Hainault. Under the auspices of these her tutelary genii the progenitrix of England's future sovereigns, was enabled to stimulate her own sex to every feminine excellence, and to soften in the other that spirit of savage ferocity which had sullied the career of the heroic monarchs of our country.

Margaret Beaufort was born in the year 1441, at Bletshoe,[1] near Higham Ferrers, the patrimonial estate of her mother, on whom had devolved the rich inheritance of the Barons Beauchamp, and whose distinguished position as sole heiress and representative of that honourable branch of the old Earls of Warwick,[2] cast additional lustre on the noble paternal lineage of this the heiress presumptive of the powerful famed Duke of Somerset.

The little Margaret was named after her mother, who was soon destined to be her sole parent, and natural guardian; as, before she had passed from infancy to childhood, she was deprived of her father's protection.

---

[1] Lysons' Mag. Britt. p. 58.
[2] Collins' Peerage, vol. iv. p. 390.

The Duke of Somerset died in the fourth year after his marriage, (27th May, 1444[1]) at the early age of thirty-nine.[*] His title, from default of male heirs, passed to his next brother, Edmunde de Beaufort, but in all besides, his daughter and only child, not quite three years old, became sole heiress to her parents' vast possessions, and to the dangers attendant upon so elevated and wealthy a station.

This distinguished warrior was interred at Wimborne Minster, in Dorset; a town for which the house of Lancaster had a particular favour,[*] and contiguous to which it is probable the parents of Margaret dwelt at the time of her father's

[1] Inquisition taken on his death.

[*] The Chronicler of Croyland (p. 519), asserts that he died by his own hand. It appears, that for some cause not explained, the duke of Somerset had incurred the displeasure of the king, and was forbidden the royal presence. "The noble heart," says the monkish historian, " of so illustrious a man took the message of this unfortunate rumour most indignantly; and not able to bear the stain of so foul a disgrace, by his own procuring he hastened his own death, choosing rather to end compendiously his present sorrow, than to pass an unhappy life in opprobrium."

Mr. Sharon Turner adopts the same view, and states positively, that he " committed suicide because courtly favour waned." (History of England, vol. iii. p. 134.) It is, however, very remarkable that so grave a circumstance should have been unnoticed by Camden, Sandford, and Dugdale, as also by Hollingshed, Fabian, Monstrellet, Walsingham, Hall, and other old chroniclers.

[*] Camden's Brit. p. 175.

decease, as Leland[1] mentions Kingeston Hall or Kingston Lacy, "a fine place," a little to the North West of Wimborne, as having appertained to John of Gaunt, and as belonging in his time to the Dukedom of Lancaster. A massive altar-tomb, erected in after years to his memory, and that of her mother, who was buried beside him, ornamented with beautiful figures of alabaster, hand in hand, attest to the present day the filial affection of their daughter.

On the decease of the Duke, the Duchess of Somerset appears to have returned to her manor in Bedfordshire; and that she resided there in great pomp for many years, may be inferred from a very ancient epitaph, formerly inscribed on the tomb of Ralph Lannoy, in the parish church of Bletshoe. He died in 1458, and is styled "Cofferer and Keeper of the Wardrobe to the most noble Margaret, Duchess of Somerset, then married to a third husband, Leo Lord Welles."[2]

In this ancient abode of the Beauchamps, and within the castellated mansion (of which vestiges are still discernible, near the farm-house which occupies the greater part of the site of the old building) did Margaret Beaufort commence that career, and pass the spring-time of that life,

[1] Leland's Itin. vol. iii. p. 71.
[2] Lyson's Mag. Brit. p. 58.

which was to produce an autumn of peace and
repose, after a summer of unexampled storm and
desolation.   But who sowed in her infant mind
those seeds of piety and virtue—who inculcated
those sound principles which actuated her conduct through life, or from what source she gained
that store of knowledge, which as regards literature was to crown her brow with laurels that
neither high birth would command, nor wealth
purchase—remains unrecorded.   Sufficient however has been handed down to posterity, to prove
that the course of instruction bestowed on the
Lady Margaret, was one very unusual for the
period in which she lived ; and that it partook
more of what was deemed essential for the
youth of the other sex than what generally fell
to the lot of females.   The Duchess of Somerset
had two sons by her first husband, Sir Oliver
St. John ; it is not, therefore, improbable, that
their tutor might also have been the preceptor
of Margaret Beaufort ; for to prevent the growth
of the tenets of Wickliffe, it had, about this
period, been made penal to put children under
private teachers,[1] so that the tutors of the high-
born youth of that age were usually the resident
confessors of the household, or churchmen from
the neighbourhood, who were famed for erudition
and sanctity.   The high state and dignity which

[1] Life of Caxton, p. 17

the Duchess is known to have maintained at her domain of Bletshoe, favours the inference, that she would engage for her children instructors of no ordinary learning and piety. That such an individual directed the opening talents of the young Margaret cannot be doubted, for it is recorded, in allusion to the austere devotion which characterized her declining years, that her education had qualified her for a studious and retired life. It is also said that she was a proficient in French, and though she was tolerably well skilled in Latin, she was often heard to complain that in her youth, she had not made herself perfect mistress of that language, which is an evident proof that the means of doing so had been afforded her, though the necessity of application seems not to have been enforced. These acquirements may appear but trivial in the existing state of knowledge ; but in forming an estimate of the advantages of education afforded to Margaret Beaufort, the proper criterion is the standard of excellence at the period in which she lived, and not that of the present day ;—a period when literature in England was at so low an ebb, that it has been recorded by Sir Thomas More, as a remarkable accomplishment in the fascinating favourite of Edward the Fourth, Jane Shore, that she could both read and write. These simple attainments, and the common rules of calculation, comprehended indeed, the entire course of instruction for persons even the most elevated in rank of the fifteenth century.[1]

The Lady Margaret must therefore, at a very early age, have given promise of that singular wisdom which in maturity won the admiration of Erasmus, and displayed that quick perception, ready wit, and extraordinary memory, which were pronounced by her exemplary confessor, the good and learned Bishop Fisher, as " passing the common rate of women."[2] By the same indisputable authority, her studious habits are made known to us, and her letters, which will be hereafter inserted in their proper places, are considered to be the most polished specimens extant of the epistolary style of her age.[3]

But though apparently associated with her half-brothers in instruction unusual for females at that time, it is nevertheless evident, that the accomplishments of her sex were not disregarded. Her knowledge of the medicinal art is particularly extolled,—an acquirement which then constituted a prominent feature in the education of the highborn female ; and she had so attentively studied even the practical department of the science, that in after years, it is recorded of her, that she devoted a portion of each day towards healing the wounds

[1] Life of Caxton, p. 17. [2] Fisher's Funeral Sermon, p. 8.
[3] Lodge, part 62.

of the indigent, and allaying by her skill the progress of their maladies. Her execution too in needle-work—almost the sole occupation and chief amusement of her sex in 'the middle ages—must have been as remarkable as her progress in more substantial acquirements; for it is related that King James the First, whenever he passed into that neighbourhood, asked to see some admirable specimens of embroidery,[1] carefully preserved in the fine old mansion of Bletshoe; and there remains to this day, in the possession of her descendants, a carpet, with the arms and alliances of the family worked by the hands of their illustrious ancestress.[2]

And well was it for the youthful Lady Margaret, that a gracious Providence had been so bountiful in its gifts to one, whom we of the present day must perceive to have been an humble instrument in the hands of her Maker, towards forwarding and bringing about those mighty changes in church and state, of which our generation are reaping the full benefit.

The great inheritance which devolved on her by her father's premature decease, had, it seems, speedily attracted the notice of the ambitious Duke of Suffolk, the favourite minister of the day; who is said to have obtained such ascen-

[1] Thoresby, Vicar. Leodensis, p. 175.
[2] Royal Wills, p. 366.

dency over the reigning monarch and his queen, that all favours passed through his hands, and his power exceeded that of all the council. He sued for and obtained a grant[1] of the wardship of the person and lands of the richly-endowed heiress,[*] while yet quite a child, but it does not appear that she was removed from the care of her mother at that early age.

The precise period when the Duchess of Somerset was united to her third husband is uncertain, but it probably occurred somewhere about the time that her illustrious daughter entered her seventh year, and may have been the plea alleged by her guardian for removing her into his own charge. Subsequent circumstances warrant also the conclusion, that it led to the removal of the Lady Margaret to the vicinity of the court, as it is stated that when she was scarcely nine years of age, the Duke of Suffolk most diligently

[1] See Appendix A.

[*] The custody of the lands of minors formed a profitable branch of the royal prerogative at this period; their wardship being either sold by the crown, or conferred on some faithful servant, or needy favourite.—Excerpta Historica, p. 111.

The Paston Letters, 55 and 56, (vol. 3,) afford a true representation of the address made use of to get possession of a rich minor, not only from the management of his estate being in the hands of the guardian, but, in order to make advantageous marriages for the families of those who were so fortunate as to obtain the care of them.

See also Testamenta Vetusta, p. 11.

sought her in marriage for John de la Pole, his
son and heir; and that his royal master, King Henry
the Sixth, wooed her at the same time for Edmund Tudor, his half-brother, better known by
the title of Earl of Richmond. The tender
age of the little heiress might seem to disprove
such an occurrence, were it not attested by authority beyond dispute—that of Lord Bacon,[1] and
her confessor, the Bishop of Rochester ; the latter
of whom, in his funeral sermon, preached at her
decease, which curious document is still extant,[*]
relates the circumstances, accompanied by the
remark, that she was by nature so acute, and her
understanding so precocious, that there was not
any thing which was too difficult for her comprehension.

The result of the rival courtship bears him out
in this statement ; but the incident which led to
so important a decision as regards her after years,
so rife with momentous events for futurity, will
be best narrated from her own account, communicated to her spiritual director. " Being then

[1] Life of Henry VII. by Lord Bacon.

[*] Entitled " A mornynge Remembrance had at the moneth
minde of the noble Prynces Margarete Countesse of Richmonde
and Darbye, moder unto Kynge Henry the Seventh, and
grandame to our Sovereign Lorde that now is." The " moneth
minde" was a monthly solemnity in memory of the deceased,
when prayers were offered and alms given for the health of
the soul.—Paston Letters, vol. iii. p. 358.

not fully nine years old, and doubtful in her mind what she were best to do, she asked counsel of an old gentlewoman, whom she much loved and trusted, which did advise her to commend herself to St. Nicholas, the patron and helper of all true maidens, and to beseech him to put in her mind what she were best to do. This counsel she followed, and made her prayer so full often, but specially that night when she should the morrow after make answer of her mind determinately. A marvellous thing! the same night, as I have heard her tell many a time, as she lay in prayer, calling upon St. Nicholas, whether sleeping or waking she could not assure, but about four of the clock in the morning, one appeared unto her arrayed like a bishop, and naming unto her, Edmund, bade take him unto her husband." [1]

This vision she related to her parents,—which warrants the inference that her mother was at this time united to Lord Welles: the supernatural direction was by them considered conclusive, and Margaret accordingly declared her preference for the king's brother, to whom she was forthwith solemnly betrothed, in accordance with the custom of that period.

The superstition which in the fifteenth century had almost usurped the place of true religion, and so alloyed the purity of prayer and supplication,

[1] Funeral Sermon, p. 9.

that miracles from pretended saints, were considered as the test of God's especial grace; renders
it by no means surprising that the over-wrought
imagination of the innocent Margaret Beaufort
should have believed that her decision had resulted
from supernatural agency. But, in the present enlightened age, when, through the blessing of God,
the spiritual tyranny of Romish priestcraft has been
swept from the land, by the force of that pure
apostolic doctrine which was beginning to manifest
itself through the immortal Wickliffe, in the
period when Margaret flourished, although not
fully matured in its powers until the days of her
grandson, King Henry the Eighth, sufficient
natural causes may be found to attach credit to
the incident. Moreover, we can discern in it,
apart from superstition, the finger of an overruling
Providence, working mysteriously, but surely,
to bring about that civil and religious emancipation
which the Almighty disposer of human events
designed should be accomplished by means of
the farther connection of the subject of this memoir with the reigning house of Lancaster.

Young as was the rich heiress of Somerset,
she had nevertheless sufficient discernment to
prefer enriching her noble kinsman ap Tudor,
rather than to gratify the ambitious and over-
bearing minister, who was already reaping so
abundant a harvest from the wardship of her great

possessions.   The comparatively recent ennoble-
ment of the De la Poles, and the fact of their
enormous wealth having been derived from mer-
cantile speculations,[1] may, in the estimation of the
great-grand-daughter of the haughty John of
Gaunt, have depreciated any advantages which
might accrue from an alliance with the family of
her guardian, when placed in comparison with the
maternal brother of the reigning monarch of
England—the grandson of Charles the Sixth of
France—the descendant of the holy and royal St.
Louis—and the lineal representative of the native
princes of Britain.

These circumstances might have influenced one
who had been reared with even less pride of birth
than the Lady Margaret; but with her education,
and at her romantic age, with the dread too of
disappointment, through the possible intrigue of
others, the image of the young Edmund Tudor,
whether she were sleeping or awake, must have
been sufficiently predominant to account for any
dream, or with the superstitious feeling of the
times, to induce the belief of an actual vision.

At this early period of our national history, the
distinctions of rank were much more strongly
marked and closely observed than in the present
day.   The nobles of the land had dealings with
those engaged in commerce, and made use of

[1] Heylyn, p. 368.

their services; but excepting on matters of business, they looked on them as a distinct race, and would have scorned to intermarry with any who moved in a sphere different from their own.[1]

Ever alive to his own advancement, the crafty Duke of Suffolk, had, in reference to this feeling, secured a powerful ally to further his ambitious views, in Edmunde de Beaufort, the uncle of his infant ward, by displacing the Duke of York in the Regency of France, and procuring the nomination, in his place, of the Duke of Somerset.[2] But the prosperity of the powerful minister was on the wane—his enemies had decreed his fall even at the moment when royal favour seemed to have fixed him on the zenith of human ambition. In February, 1449, articles of impeachment[3] were exhibited against him by the house of commons; and the king, to appease them, committed him to the Tower, (28th Hen. VI.) One of the leading accusations was that of having united his youthful ward, the Lady Margaret, with John de la Pole, his heir, immediately prior to his arrest, with the view to her being a claimant of the throne of England in case Henry the Sixth had no issue. This charge in its full extent appears however to have been groundless, although the unpopular minister might probably have incau-

[1] Paston Letters, vol. iv.   [2] Baker's Chron. 187.
[3] Paston Letters, vol. iii. p. 63.

tiously avowed his intention of securing to his
family the riches and alliance of the young
heiress of Somerset, by a compulsory betrothment
to his eldest son.* The duke was released through
the influence of the queen, after a brief imprisonment. Within a few weeks, however, his un-
popularity threatened such serious consequences,
that Henry the Sixth, at the instigation of the
Commons, banished him to Calais for five years;
but he was treacherously seized on his voyage
thither by spies, and cruelly murdered at sea, the
2nd May, 1450. These proceedings of Parliament have, however, led many into the error of
believing, that Margaret Beaufort's first husband
was the duke's eldest son. Her statement respecting the vision of St. Nicholas wholly sets at
rest any suspicion of the alleged marriage; and
besides the infantine age of the parties, the important fact of the stigma which would have
attached to the birth of Henry the Seventh, as
also to the children of John de la Pole, who
eventually married the sister of King Edward the
Fourth, would fully confirm her testimony that
she was wooed by the king and his minister at

* The power of disposing of a ward in marriage, when under
the direction of a covetous or bad guardian, was often most
shamefully abused; and tyrannical as it was, it continued in
force till the reign of Charles the Second.—See Paston Letters, vol. iii. p. 227.

the same time, " though not fully nine years old."

A still more conclusive refutation of the charge is presented in the beautiful and affecting letter *

* This interesting document is here inserted, on account of its own merits, and because it emanated from the pen of the guardian of the illustrious subject of this Memoir.

" My dear and only well-beloved Son,

" I beseech our Lord in Heaven, the maker of all the world, to bless you, and to send you ever grace to love him and to dread him, to the which, as far as a father may charge his child, I both charge you, and pray you, to set all your spirits and wits to do and to know his holy laws and commandments, by the which ye shall, with his great mercy, pass all the tempests and troubles of this wretched world: and that also, wittingly, ye do nothing for love nor dread of any earthly creature, that should displease Him. And there as [whenever] any frailty maketh you fall, beseech his mercy soon to call you to him again with repentance, satisfaction, and contrition of your heart, never more in will to offend him. Secondly, next Him, above all earthly things, to be true liegeman in heart, in will, in thought, in deed, unto the king, our aldermost [greatest] high and dread sovereign lord, to whom both ye and I be so much bound to; charging 'you, as father can and may, rather to die than to be the contrary, or to know any thing that were against the welfare or prosperity of his most royal person; but that as far as your body and life may stretch, ye live and die to defend it, and to let his highness have knowledge thereof in all the haste ye can. Thirdly, in the same wise, I charge you, my dear son, alway as ye be bounden by the Commandment of God to do, to love, to worship your lady and mother; and also that ye obey alway her commandments, and to believe her counsels and advices in all your works, the which dread not but shall be best and truest to you. And if any other body would stir you to the contrary, to flee the

written by the ill-fated nobleman to his son, the day before he left England ; in which, though his several duties to his God, his king, and his mother, are solemnly enforced, no mention whatever is made of his obligations as a husband.

Nevertheless, at the time when she was sought in marriage by her royal and noble suitors, which was some months previous to the tragical death of her

counsel in any wise, for ye shall find it naught and evil. Furthermore, as far as father may and can, I charge you in any wise to flee the company and counsel of proud men, of covetous men, and of flattering men, the more especially and mightily to withstand them, and not to draw nor to meddle with them with all your might and power; and to draw to you, and to your company, good and virtuous men, and such as be of good conversation and of truth, and by them shall ye never be deceived nor repent you of. Moreover, never follow your own wit in no wise, but in all your works, of such folks as I write of above ask your advice and counsel, and doing thus, with the mercy of God, ye shall do right well, and live in right much worship and great heart's rest and ease. And I will be to you as good lord and father as my heart can think. And last of all, as heartily and as lovingly as ever father blessed his child on earth, I give you the blessing of our Lord and of me, which of his infinite mercy increase you in all virtue and good living; and that your blood may by his grace from kindred to kindred, multiply in this earth to his service in such wise as, after the departing from this wretched world here, ye and they may glorify him eternally amongst his angels in Heaven.

Written of mine hand,

The day of my departing from this land,

Your true and loving father,

April 28*th,* 1450.   SUFFOLK."

Paston Letters, vol. i. p. 32.

guardian, the youthful Margaret and her aged
friend well knew she would be allowed no actual
choice of suitors, though the decision might nominally rest with her; and the spirit of romance
which tinctured the moral actions, no less than the
ascetic bigotry which marked the spiritual views
of that period, might have led her adviser, from a
well-meaning zeal, to impose some deception upon
the innocent and guileless creature, who, with her
worldly inclinations still bent towards Edmund
Tudor, was evidently desirous of leaving to heavenly direction the future path of her earthly career.
That Margaret Beaufort believed she saw a vision,
is beyond all doubt; but whether she was deceived
into the belief by the agency of others, or whether
her childish imagination dwelt on St. Nicholas in
prayer, until his image, and the object of her
wishes were associated in her dreams, cannot be
decided; and would indeed be a most unimportant
point, had not the circumstance led to a result, so
fraught with momentous events, as the marriage
to which it was the prelude.

Some few years, however, elapsed before the
union of this illustrious young couple; and as the
interval contains no historical facts connected with
the Lady Margaret, which demand particular
attention, it affords a fitting opportunity to trace
the parentage of her future husband. This is the
more needed as the Royal lineage of Edmund

Tudor increased the perils and vicissitudes to
which her own noble descent exposed this distinguished scion of the Red Rose of Lancaster,—
that ill-omened badge which seemed to encircle
with thorns the footsteps of all who cherished the
fatal flower,—the crimsoned leaves of which were
reddened yet more deeply by the blood of friends
and relatives,—whose root sprang from usurpation
and regicide, —whose opening buds were germs
of discord, — whose expanded blossoms were sig-
nals of destruction.   It is with feelings of repose
that the mind, passing from such harrowing scenes,
rests on the gentle character whose descent en-
tailed not upon her the destructive qualities of
her race.   No ! she was the flower that was destined to survive the blight which eventually visited
her family ; and to perpetuate, by means of her
good deeds, that line which valour, heroism, and
undaunted courage, had raised indeed to the
highest pinnacle of glory, but which that very
success tended only the more speedily to anni-
hilate.

At the commencement of this Memoir, and
when tracing the connection of Margaret Beaufort
with the blood-royal of England, Henry the
Fourth, eldest son of John of Gaunt, was mentioned as being established on the throne of England, after its usurpation from his cousin Richard
the Second.   He was succeeded by his son Henry

the Fifth; who, at the treaty of Melun, was so
fascinated by the surpassing loveliness of Katherine, only daughter of Charles the Sixth of
France, who had been brought thither with the
view of attracting the renowned monarch, that,
though the vanquisher of her father's kingdom,
he solicited and obtained the daughter in marriage. His domestic happiness, however, was as
brief as his reign was glorious, for he survived
his marriage only two years, leaving his beautiful
widow scarcely of age, with a son but a few
months old, who was proclaimed king, by the
title of Henry the Sixth, and surnamed " of
Windsor," from the place of his birth.

But this illustrious princess, regarded as dowager-queen both of France and England, by reason
of her husband having borne the title of King of
both realms, was destined ere long, in her turn,
to bow at the conquering shrine of personal
attractions. She became so enamoured with
Owen ap Tudor, a Welsh gentleman, of moderate
fortune, though ancient family, who was attending
the court at Windsor, that unmindful of her high
estate, and following only the impulse of attachment, she was privately united to him, on her
son's entering his seventh year.[1] This alliance
excited great indignation, as well as astonishment;
that a brow which had been graced with the lily,

[1] Baker's Chron. p. 180.

and crowned with the rose, could disregard the
regal circlet, and condescend to become the bride
of a private individual—a mere soldier of fortune.
To the princes of the realm, who ruled during the
minority of the young king, the marriage was so
offensive, that a law was forthwith passed, enacting
severe penalties on any person who might pre-
sume to espouse the Dowager-Queen of England,
without the license of the reigning monarch.[1]
But the slenderness of Ap Tudor's fortune, and
the mean extraction imputed to him by his enemies,[2] was more than counterbalanced, in Queen
Catherine's estimation, by his noble bearing and
extraordinary personal endowments.

Owen ap Tudor, however, though the victim of
calumny and prejudice, was not unworthy of alliance
with the British empire. He could justly boast of
two royal descents, and claimed higher lineage even,
than that of the Fleur-de-lys of France, or the
Planta-Genista of England. Accumulated reverses had greatly reduced his parents from the
dignified station, which was nevertheless their
birth-right; for in virtue of their ancestry, he
claimed uninterrupted descent from the aboriginal princes of Britain,[3] through Arthur and Uther
Pendragon, the grandsons of Constantine the

---

[1] Cotton's Abridgment of Parl. Records, p. 589.
[2] Sandford's Geneal. vol. iv. p. 7.
[3] Pennant's Wales, p. 257.

Great, whose British dominions (A.D. 310.) were
united to the empire of Rome, of which he was
the first Christian emperor.[1] In proof of his
direct descent from Cadwallader, the last British
prince, and first King of Wales, (A.D. 678.) he
bore a dragon as his device, that being the ensign
of the above-named ancient monarch, and was
consequently displayed by the grandson of Owen
ap Tudor, King Henry the Seventh, on his victorious standard at the battle of Bosworth Field.[2]
Leaving it to antiquaries to decide the merits
of this lengthened pedigree, it will be sufficient
here to state the fact, that, in 1428,[3] the beautiful
Queen Mother, the Princess Katherine of France,
became the acknowledged wife of Owen ap Tudor;
and many ludicrous tales are still extant arising
from this incongruous union.[4]

The issue of their marriage was three sons and
one daughter, viz. Edmund Tudor, surnamed of
Hadham, his royal mother's manor-house, and the
place of his birth ; Jasper Tudor, denominated of
Hatfield, another manor-house appertaining to
Queen Katherine, where he was born ; Owen
Tudor, who early embraced a monastic life ; and
Katherine Tudor, who died young.[5]

From some cause which has not transpired, the

---

[1] Heylyn, p. 16. [2] Granger, p. 28.
[3] Rym. Fed. x. p. 662. [4] Hist. of Gwyder Family, p. 69.
[5] Dugdale's Baron. tom. ii.

illustrious Katherine, in a few years, separated
from her husband; and taking refuge in the
monastery of Bermondsey, in Southwark,[1] she
there died, at the age of thirty-eight, in the year
1437. She was buried at Westminster, by the
side of her royal consort, Henry the Fifth. Her
second husband survived her many years, but paid
a heavy penalty for his regal alliance, as immediately after Katherine's decease, he was seized
and imprisoned in Newgate, for his presumption
in espousing the Queen dowager.[2] His sons were
forthwith taken from him, but out of respect
for the memory of their royal mother, they were
placed under the tutelage of Katherine de la
Pole, Abbess of Barking.[3] Owen ap Tudor,
eventually effected his escape, but was a second
time seized; and a series of persecutions and
imprisonments marked the remainder of his
chequered career. Having at length been released, by command of Henry the Sixth, he
devoted himself zealously to his cause; and after
distinguishing himself in various conflicts, was
taken prisoner, with his second son, Jasper,
bravely fighting at Mortimer's Cross; and in the
last year of that monarch's eventful reign, was
beheaded by the Yorkist faction at Hereford,
and there buried in 1461.[4]

[1] Sandford Gen. chap. 9.   [2] Rymer Fed. x. p. 228.
[3] Rymer Fed. ibid.   [4] Holinsh. Chron. p. 660.

Such is the history of the immediate ancestors of Edmund Tudor, to whom Margaret Beaufort was betrothed at the early age of nine years; a history so replete with romantic adventure, that it orms a suitable appendage to the vision of St. Nicholas, and is rendered yet more striking as a tale of the marvellous, because her union with the descendant of the first rulers of Britain, led to the accomplishment of the prophecies of Merlin, whose predictions had been regarded as oracles, not only by the bards, who recited his mysterious traditions, but also by kings and nobles, who for many generations had listened devoutly to the legendary lore of Merlin's prophecy delivered to Vortigern,—of his magical aid afforded to Uther, — of the wonderful exploits of King Arthur, and the knights of the round table,—and in short, to fabulous narrations of all the native princes of Britain, down to Cadwallader of Wales, from whom Edmund Tudor claimed, as already observed, uninterrupted descent, and whose progeny Merlin had declared should one day regain the dominion of the land.[1]

King Henry the Sixth, when old enough to assume the reins of government, had not been content with merely releasing, so soon as he could effect it, his father-in-law from imprisonment, but he testified in the most amiable and affectionate

[1] Camden's Brit. vol. i. p. 2.

manner his kindness and love for his maternal
brothers, who were about ten years younger than
himself. He had them carefully educated, under
the most honest and virtuous ecclesiastics;[1] and
when of an age to be removed to court, they are
noticed as in attendance on the king and queen.
In the year 1452, Margaret of Anjou, who then
came to Norwich with the view of raising troops,
is particularly stated to have been attended by the
king's half-brothers, Edmund of Hadham, and
Jasper of Hatfield. It has been already stated
how early he interested himself for the former, by
endeavouring to secure for his future bride the
wealthy heiress of Somerset. The year following
their betrothment, he bestowed on him the castle
and county of Richmount, or Richmondshire, in
the North-Riding of York, creating him at the
same time, by letters patent, Earl of Richmond,
with this peculiar privilege, that he should take
precedence above all earls, and sit in parliament
next to dukes, by reason of his near consanguinity
to the reigning monarch.[3] His brother, Jasper
Tudor, in the same year, 1452, he advanced to
the dignity of Earl of Pembroke,[4] by which he
became possessed of the castle and royal territories

[1] Blakman Collect. p. 229.

[2] Paston Letters, vol. i. p. 68.

[3] Rot. Parl. 32 H. VI. m. 12.

[4] Lords' Report on the Dignity of the Peerage, vol. ix.
p. 231.

in South Wales, appertaining to the title, the
earldom having been erected into a county Pala-
tine in 1138; also of the ancient mansion in
the metropolis, belonging to the Earldom of
Pembroke, a fine building, then denominated
Pembroke's Inn, now known as Stationers' Hall.
In addition to these honours, the Earl of Richmond shortly afterwards obtained from the
monarch, a grant in fee, of the noble mansion
called Baynard's Castle,[1] situate near Paul's
Wharf, on the banks of the Thames; which
had recently been enlarged and beautified by
Humphrey Duke of Gloucester, the king's uncle;
on whose death without issue, it fell to the crown,
and was bestowed by Henry upon his brother.
Here it is probable the young Earl of Richmond chiefly sojourned, during the interval that
elapsed prior to his marriage, this palace of the
Saxon kings being usually occupied by some near
connection of the crown.

To return, however, to the young heiress, of
Somerset; who, at the time of her betrothment,
though a child in years, had proved herself far
above a child in understanding, and whose personal
history will now be resumed, at a period usually
allotted to the happy carelessness of girlhood. But
with Margaret Beaufort, times and seasons appear
to have been anticipated, in all the leading inci-

[1] Polydore Virgil, 522, n. 10.

dents of her remarkable career, and ere the
maiden's timidity had fully checked the sprightli-
ness of youth, she was called on to assume the
duties and responsibilities of a matron. She had
been instructed to believe, that it was the fitting
season to fulfil the vows made in her childish days,
and so singularly gifted was she by nature, that
her character and qualifications needed not the
accompaniment of age, to fit her for the important station she was henceforth to occupy.

On this matter there is no doubt, nor any necessity to rely on mere inference. The annals of
her time, and the testimony of contemporaries,
assure us, that in " manners she was right noble,
as in blood,"[1] and that her personal endowments were fully equal to her illustrious descent.
That she was dignified in demeanour, courteous
in speech, gentle in disposition, patient, generous,
obedient, and humble ; neither revengeful nor
cruel, but ready to bury in forgetfulness the greatest injuries ; charitable to the poor, and pitiful of
their sufferings ; mindful of the slightest kindness,
easy of access, and full of tenderness to all who
were allied to her. Above all things, she was devoted to her God, beseeching his mercy, with an
innate fervour of piety, far above her tender age,
and very uncommon, at a period when outward
form and display was mistaken for inward piety.

[1] Funeral Sermon, p. 5.

Distrusting herself, and with the fear of His
judgments ever before her, she would daily, with
an intensity of devotion, that proved her safe-
guard through life, prostrate herself before the
throne of grace, early in the morning, and at mid-
day, seeking with prayer and supplication humbly, but fervently, from the Omniscient Creator
and disposer of human events, guidance for the
young and inexperienced creature, who wept and
knelt before Him.

In short, to quote once more the words of her
spiritual confessor, whose situation, by reason of
the religious practice of the times, enabled him,
in the awful secrecy of the confessional, to read
every virtue, and search out every vice: "she
had, in a manner, all that was praisable in a woman, either in soul or body."[1] Her enthusiastic
ardour, for the rescue of the Holy Land from the
infidels, almost amounted to fanaticism, yet was
it tempered by so much humility, that she would
often say, if the princes of Christendom would
combine, and march against the Turks, she would
willingly attend the camp in some menial capacity.[2]
So accordant indeed were her actions with her
professions—so beautifully did she blend the moral
with the religious virtues, that Dr. Fuller has justly
observed, " She was a pattern of the best devotion of her times."[3]

<hr>

[1] Funeral Sermon. p. 6.   [2] Camden's Remains. p. 271.

Such was Margaret Beaufort, when, in her fifteenth year, she exchanged her simple maiden name, for the more lofty title of Countess of Richmond. She was united to the young Earl in 1455,[1] and, by means of this union, it is remarkable that she became allied by birth or marriage to no less than thirty kings and queens within the fourth degree either of blood or affinity.[2] Edmund Tudor had just entered his twenty-fifth year, and having been the object of her especial choice, sanctified too as that choice was by her firm conviction that she was influenced by a higher source, the youthful Lady Margaret entered the married state with brighter prospects of happiness than usually fell to the lot of persons of distinction at that period, on account of the forced and early matches so prevalent in the middle ages.[3]

With an imagination peculiarly fitted to delight in the wild and romantic legends connected with her husband's pedigree, and with her memory well stored, owing to her studious habits, with the poetry of an age, when the "gay science" of minstrelsy was in its highest prosperity—we find her, as was naturally to be expected, accompanying the Earl of Richmond, shortly after their union to the land of his ancestors. Their chief

---

[1] Rot. Parl. v. 343.   [2] Funeral Sermon, p. 7.
[3] Paston Letters, v. iii. p. 227.

abode appears to have been Pembroke Castle in
South Wales, the princely domain of their brother Jasper Tudor, Earl of Pembroke.   Here, in
this land of daring enterprise, and determined
patriotism, Margaret of Richmond, about a twelve-
month after her marriage, namely, on St. Anne's
day, the 26th of July, 1456, gave birth to a son and
heir.   In the most ancient portion of the noble fortress above-mentioned, and in a chamber, which the
antiquary Leland visited, and minutely describes,
the youthful Countess, became a parent, and in
the infant Henry of Richmond, she welcomed a
fresh tie to that being on whom she had early
bestowed her heart's best and purest affections.

But alas ! her cup of happiness was full ! full
even to overflowing ; and ere the bridal chaplet
had faded from her brow, Margaret was called on
to drink as deeply of the bitterness of grief, as
she had prematurely been permitted to taste the
plenitude of earthly felicity.   Before the second
year of her nuptials had expired, the mother's
smiles were changed for the widow's tears.   The
Earl of Richmond, in the prime of life, in the
full enjoyment of all that this world deems great
and prosperous, was summoned to a premature
grave.   He died on the 1st November, 1456,
leaving the bereaved Margaret, herself only in
her sixteenth year, with an infant son,[1] the in-

[1] Dugdale's Baron. vol. ii. p. 239.

heritor of the earldom, which his father had not enjoyed above four years, and destined to become in right of his mother, (though the knowledge thereof was hidden by the veil of futurity), the future monarch of England.

His illustrious parent was buried in the church of the Grey Friars at Caermarthen, from whence his remains, upon the suppression of the abbey, were removed to the cathedral of St. David's.[1] In the centre of the choir, and beneath a monument directly before the steps of the high altar, they yet lie, with an inscription styling him "Father and brother to kings."[2]

But the vigorous and well-disciplined mind of Margaret of Richmond was singularly calculated to endure the extremity of grief. Deeply embued with religious zeal, her faith was too firmly rooted to be shaken by the blast of affliction. She could discern the chastening hand of the Almighty from the arm of the avenger; and though smitten to the heart's core, and that too in the very zenith of her joy, she could school

[1] Sandford's Geneal. Hist. B. iv. ch. 9.

[2] The Earl of Richmond was buried in the chancel of the church of St. David's, with this inscription upon his monument: "Under this marble stone, here enclosed, rest the bones of that noble lord, Edmund, Earl of Richmond, father and brother to Kings; who departed out of this world in the year 1456: the first day of November. On whose soul Almighty Jesu have mercy."—Master's Memoirs of Thomas Baker, p. 149.

her grief sufficiently to feel, that she had duties
to perform to the living, which were yet more
binding, from being hallowed by her fond remembrance of the dead. On her infant and now
orphan child, the offspring of short-lived but genuine attachment, the Lady Margaret henceforth
bestowed as much of her devotion and affection,
as she tremblingly thought could be spared from
the service of her God. Her struggles indeed were
great, but her fortitude never forsook her; and with
a submissive spirit, that brought its own reward,
the widowed Countess tutored herself to feel, with
true Christian piety, that while her infant son
was spared she was not wholly bereft. How long
that blessing might be hers, she feared to think—
for his sickly constitution during infancy was a
fresh source of affliction to his anxious mother;
but Richmond's earliest biographer, Bernard Andreas, who was contemporary with him, — and
from whose authority this fact is derived * —
bears testimony also to the maternal solicitude of
the Lady Margaret, who nursed and tended her

* Bernard Andreas was a native of Toulouse, and an Au-
gustine monk; he was poet laureate to Henry VII. and his
son Henry VIII. and was prince Arthur's tutor in grammar.
His unpublished life of Henry VII. is in the Cottonian
MSS. (Dom. xviii.) and was written in 1509. He was made
poet laureate in the 11th Henry VII. 1486, with an annuity
of 10 marks; and in the privy purse expences of that monarch,
(Excerpta Hist. p. 115.) frequent mention is made of small
sums given "To the blynde poet in rewarde."

puny offspring with a watchfulness and care, more in unison with her energetic character than her youthful age.

The period in which this heavy loss, so early blighted the fair prospects of the Lady Margaret, was one fraught with peculiar misery to England, and more especially with imminent political danger to her own, and her late husband's family. The Earl of Richmond, as already observed, expired in 1456, an era memorable in our annals, in consequence of Richard Plantagenet, Duke of York, having been made Protector of the King's person, and of the realm.[1] From the opposition made to this nomination, by the Queen and Lancastrian party,[2] and the foundation which these conflicting interests laid, for those fearful civil wars, between the partizans of the Red and White Roses, to the former of which, by birth and marriage, the Lady Margaret of Richmond was so closely allied.

Her uncle and nearest paternal relative, Edmund Duke of Somerset had been slain at the battle of St. Alban's, a short time before, bravely fighting for Henry the Sixth, and endeavouring to check the growing power of the House of York,[3] and the Earl of Pembroke, her husband's brother, and her child's natural guardian, in whose castle

[1] Rot. Parl. V. 284. [2] Baker's Chron. p. 94.
[3] Harleian MSS. 545.

too she was sojourning, was one of the most determined enemies of the protector and his party, and an equally strenuous supporter of his kinsman, the reigning monarch.

With a prudence and foresight, which seemed inherent in her character, Margaret saw the necessity of avoiding all contact with the contending parties. Keeping far aloof from the vicinity of the court, she resolved on continuing her abode in Pembrokeshire; a step well calculated to shield both herself and her infant son from those perils, which might possibly ensue, in consequence of the nation being on the verge of a civil war.

Built on a rock, and nearly encompassed by water as was Jasper Tudor's fortress, she was at least secure from sudden attacks; and she judiciously considered, that the grandson of Owen Tudor — the descendant of the native princes of Britain,—would be better protected in Wales, than the aspect of public affairs promised for the nephew of the reigning sovereign, either at his own castle of Richmond, or in any other part of distracted England.

Few buildings selected by necessity, could have been better suited for the nursery of royalty, than Pembroke Castle. Of Norman architecture with a mixture of the early Gothic, it had been rendered in every respect a residence suitable to princes, by the first Earl of Pembroke, the re-

nowned Gilbert de Clare, surnamed Strongbow,
who becoming possessed of the royal territories
in that quarter, had strengthened it with such
additional fortifications, as, added to its remarkable keep or tower, rendered it one of the most
majestic edifices in Britain. Here the Countess
of Richmond continued to reside[1] for many succeeding years, studiously instilling into the mind
of her son, those precepts of religion and morality
— that supporting confidence in his God — that
power of self-endurance — that contempt of danger, which shone forth so conspicuously in his
after-life, and which have been universally ascribed
by all his biographers to the admirable tuition
bestowed on him by his exemplary and judicious
mother.

Far removed from political excitement, and
thus engaged with her religious and maternal
duties, it is here necessary again to digress from
the narrative of her peculiar history, and leave the
Lady Margaret to take a wider survey of the historical events of the time. Her private career
being so intimately blended with public affairs,
it becomes essential to a clear understanding of
the former occasionally to retrace the latter, that
it may more clearly appear how entirely the vicissitudes of her chequered life arose from her connection with the political events of the age.

[1] Fenton, p. 462.

The vicissitudes of Margaret Beaufort were of
no common kind. On her they pressed heavily
and fearfully; in us they excite an overwhelming
interest, as the harbingers of bright and glorious
results, gradually, but *now* fully accomplished.
It is on occasions such as these, when we have
the opportunity of studying the human character
under the influence of peculiar trial—of contem-
plating humanity under all the modifications of
good and evil — of judging of man's powers of
resistance and endurance, and perceiving the influence which local circumstances and physical
causes exercise over all ages and conditions, that
we learn the true value, and real character of historical research. We fulfil not its design when
we limit our attention to the collections of the
mere annalist, and exercise our memory, by
stringing together, dates and details, without
pausing to profit by the moral truths they incul-
cate.

The history of nations — the rise and fall of
empires, — the extinction or degeneracy of once
powerful states, enlarge our views by linking past
ages with more enlightened times, and enable
us to trace the gradual advance of civil, intellectual, and legislative improvement. But it is the
study of man alone, which exercises the higher
faculties of our reason. This teaches us to form
a true estimate of persons and things, stimulates

the noblest powers of the mind, and calls forth
the best, the purest, and the most generous feelings of our nature. The one speaks to our understanding and feeds the pride of human knowledge, the other acts upon the heart, and teaches
us how limited is our power, and how little capable we are of selecting our own path.

Few periods in the history of any nation, have
been more fraught with striking results than the
close of the fifteenth century, not merely to our
own country, but to far distant and at that time
undiscovered lands ; but whose inhabitants have
since been freed from debasing slavery as were
England's sons from religious thraldom, a deliverance arising from causes, which had their rise in
this remarkable era, and of which the subject of
this memoir by the wise counsels and judicious
instruction early bestowed on Henry of Richmond
was the active, though unconscious agent. Hence
we are led, of necessity, from the contemplation
of her own striking character, to those political
events and national benefits with which it is inseparably united, and which have shed an enduring
halo round the name of Margaret Beaufort.

The last historical summary left Henry the
Sixth on the throne of England, to which it will
be remembered he succeeded, while yet quite an
infant. A long minority was the obvious result
of his father's early decease, and this was guarded

by one of the wisest and most efficient regencies
that this, or any other country ever possessed.

Had the illustrious son of the valiant conqueror
of France succeeded to dominion at a riper age,
the long catalogue of miseries, which marked his
eventful reign, might possibly have been averted
both from his country and himself.[1]   But his title
to the throne of England, being no other than
that of a continued usurpation from Henry the
Fourth, and his claim to that of France, the
result of the treaty of Troye, in direct opposition to the natural rights of the Dauphin,
the legal heir of that kingdom, it was scarcely
within the power of the ablest regency to maintain undisputed the succession of a monarch
who with such doubtful titles, was proclaimed
king of England at the age of nine months, and
king of France before he had attained his second
year.

Nevertheless, with a spirit of integrity, which
has called forth the approbation of succeeding
ages, his two uncles, by consent of parliament,[2]
promptly undertook and ably fulfilled the trust
reposed in them by their brother, the deceased
monarch, who by his will had delegated the
regency of France to John, the brave Duke of
Bedford ; and under the title of Lord Protector,

[1] Sharon Turner, vol. iii. p. 135.
[2] Parl. Rolls. v. p. 174.

the government of England, to Humphrey, the amiable Duke of Gloucester, who was both learned himself, and a great patron of literature. The guardianship of the young king's person had been committed to Thomas, Duke of Exeter, his great uncle, (youngest son of John of Gaunt,) whose actions were graced equally with judgment, valour, and discretion. These, with the addition of Cardinal Beaufort,—to whose zeal were entrusted the ecclesiastical labours of the cabinet,— guided the helm of state, during the minority of Henry the Sixth, and so long as he continued a child in years, his dominions were kept flourishing by the provident measures of his careful and vigilant uncles. They so faithfully discharged the duties respectively assigned them, and evinced such ability in their several offices, that although their administration was carried on chiefly by force of arms and rigorous enactments, they, nevertheless, secured for their nephew the love and loyalty of his subjects, and maintained both his kingdoms in a most prosperous and happy condition. Upon attaining his eighth year, he was crowned King of England, at Westminster, in 1429, and in the year following by a repetition of the same solemn ceremony at Paris, he received the oaths, and fealty of the French nobility, as sovereign of that realm.[1]

[1] Baker's Chron. p. 184.

But unhappily for the country at large, and especially for the faction of which he was the head, Henry of Lancaster was fitter for an ecclesiastic than a King. His disposition was too gentle for the warlike period in which he lived, and his nature too placid to oppose with sufficient vigour the turbulence of his enemies, who, while they admired his virtues, availed themselves of his weakness to gratify their ambition, and to work his destruction. The extreme severity exercised by his tutor, the zealous and chivalric Earl of Warwick,[1] had a tendency to break the spirit which it was his object to kindle in his meek and docile pupil, while the continued struggles for political ascendancy which gradually arose between the Duke of Gloucester and Cardinal Beaufort, by excluding the young monarch, even at the age of seventeen,[2] from all participation in a government to which he should early have been admitted, enfeebled still more the naturally inactive and too yielding disposition of the unfortunate Henry the Sixth.

As soon as he was of sufficient age to take upon himself the executive power, his incapacity for ruling was evinced by dissensions at home, and losses abroad. His misfortunes began early, by reason of the death of his able

---

[1] Paston Letters, vol. iii. p. 12.

[2] Rot. Parl. v. 433, and Paston Letters, vol. iii. p. 12.

and judicious uncle, the Duke of Bedford; and
were completed by his ill-assorted union, in direct
opposition to the Duke of Gloucester's policy,
with Margaret of Anjou,[1] a princess who brought
him no strength of alliance, and but small dowry;
but who possessed an ambition so inordinate, and
a spirit so masculine and daring, that, stimulated as
it was by the intriguing spirit of her favourite the
Duke of Suffolk, (the early guardian of Margaret
Beaufort,) it embroiled her husband in a constant
succession of private quarrels and destructive warfare. Her imperious manner and unconciliating
disposition gradually alienated from the king the
love of his friends; and the cruel murder of his only
surviving uncle the excellent Duke of Gloucester,
presumptive heir to the crown,—usually ascribed to
agents employed by Cardinal Beaufort, the queen,
and the Duke of Suffolk,[2]—completed his unpo-
pularity with his subjects; who soon grew impatient
at the slavish superstition to which Henry the
Sixth unhappily devoted himself, and disgusted
at the want of energy which permitted him to be
governed by a woman, and to leave the affairs of
state solely to the guidance of his heroic but
injudicious consort. The severe trials of this
unhappy princess have stifled, in succeeding generations, all feelings but those of commiseration
and pity. The joyous welcome which greeted

[1] Fabian, 440.   [2] Paston Letters, vol. iii. p. 6.

her on landing in England, and the rejoicings
which followed her marriage, formed a striking
and melancholy contrast to the sorrows of her
after years. The poems of Lydgate have trans-
mitted to posterity the graces and attractions which
he so lavishly praises, and contemporary chroniclers corroborate Hall's assertion, that she " ex-
celled all other in beauty and favour, as well as
in wit and policy."[1] Whatever may have been
her failings, her maternal love, her disregard of
personal privations, and her undaunted courage
in the hour of danger, were the theme of admiration and astonishment at the period in which she
flourished, and have commanded the respect and
sympathy of posterity.

On the death of the Duke of Suffolk, whose
cruel murder has been already noticed, the Duke
of Somerset, uncle to the Countess of Richmond,
succeeded as Prime Minister of England, and
enjoyed equally with his predecessor the regal
favour and confidence.[2] His strong influence
over the queen, however, and the despotic power
which he exercised, contributed to render him no
less unpopular, than that ill-fated nobleman;
and the melancholy aberration of intellect, which
for the space of nearly two years reduced Henry

[1] Hall's Chron. p. 205.
[2] Paston Letters, vol. iii. p. 110.

the Sixth to a state of lethargic idiotcy,[1] formed a pretext which was gladly seized by parliament for removing the obnoxious minister.

Richard Plantagenet, Duke of York, was nominated regent and defender of the realm,[2] and the Duke of Somerset, after being arrested almost in the queen's presence, was committed a prisoner to the Tower. This proceeding gave rise to a spirit of bitterness between the partizans of the two noblemen, which never afterwards could be softened; and the unlooked-for recovery of the king, with the consequent ascendancy of the queen and her favourite the Duke of Somerset, produced the most disastrous results to the country. The De Beauforts, of which family the Duke of Somerset became the head, by the death of the Lady Margaret's father without male issue, assumed to be the representatives of the Lancastrian line, in the event of Henry the Sixth dying without children, and so without doubt they were; for though the Duke of York was the legal heir to the throne by descent from Edward the Third, the De Beauforts were the nearest relatives of the reigning monarch and his immediate ancestors, whose sovereignty had been recognized by parliament, and who had swayed the British sceptre for nearly fifty years.

---

[1] Rot. Parl. v. p. 241.   [2] Rot. Parl. v. p. 242.

But on the other hand the claims of the House of York were founded in strict justice, though they took their rise at a period antecedent; one, which it will be recollected gave occasion to a former historical digression in this memoir, and the object of which was to show the relative position of the De Beauforts with the royal family at the period of the Lady Margaret's birth. The crown of England, as then stated, was placed in the House of Lancaster, by the usurpation of Henry the Fourth, the offspring of John of Gaunt, fourth son of Edward the Third. The monarch he deposed—Richard the Second, heir to that king's eldest son, the Black Prince,—left no issue; and William of Hatfield, the second son, died unmarried; but Lionel, Duke of Clarence, King Edward's third son, had an only daughter, Philippa, who became the lawful heir of the crown; and the right of her descendants was indisputably superior to that of the children of John of Gaunt, who was a younger brother.* But

* The substance of the Duke of York's claim to the crown of England was as follows: — "King Edward the Third had seven sons. 1. Edward, Prince of Wales. 2. William of Hatfield. 3. Lionel, Duke of Clarence. 4. John of Gaunt, Duke of Lancaster. 5. Edmund, Duke of York. 6. Thomas, Duke of Gloucester, and 7. William of Windsor. Edward the eldest died during his father's life time, and left one son, King Richard the Second, who died without issue, as also did King Edward's second son, William. Lionel, the third son, had only one daughter, named Philippa, who being married to Ed-

Henry of Bolingbroke, having forcibly obtained
possession of the throne, continued to retain it
by the sword, and the brilliant reign of his son
Henry the Fifth, made him so popular with his
subjects, that it rendered any opposition from the
descendants of Philippa of Clarence utterly futile.

Far different was the case when the meek and
inactive successor of such warlike ancestors came
to inherit the possessions which their valour had
acquired and maintained. The grievances which
multiplied yearly, and the gradual diminution of
our French possessions arising from the king's
misgovernment, and that of his ministry, induced
the more warlike portion of the community to
consider the slender claims of the ancestors of
Henry the Sixth to a sovereignty for which their
descendant was so evidently unfitted. The spirit
of discontent once roused, spread with incon-
ceivable rapidity, and the majority of the kingdom were soon divided into two powerful factions;
the one favouring the weak but amiable representative of the valorous House of Lancaster,
then on the throne; the other advocating the re-

mund Mortimer, Earl of March, she had by him Roger, Earl of
March, who afterwards had two sons and two daughters, of
whom three died without issue, and Anne, the sole heiress
married Richard, Earl of Cambridge, the son of Edmund,
Duke of York, the fifth son of King Edward the Third;
which Earl of Cambridge was father of Richard, Duke of York,
the present claimant.

storation of the rightful heirs, whose claims were
at this period centred in Richard Plantagenet,
Duke of York, a prince as eminent for his private
virtues, as he was distinguished for his heroism
and wisdom.

The state of imbecility under which the king
laboured, taken in conjunction with the unexpected appearance of an heir to the throne,
about ten years after his union with Margaret of
Anjou,[1] and after the rights of the protector had
been recognised by parliament, contributed more
than all else to give a preponderance to the claims
of the House of York, from the suspicions of
legitimacy which attached to the birth of the
young prince.

The noble duke above named united, in his
own person, two branches of the posterity of
Edward the Third. His parents being brothers'
children, he was the descendant on the father's
side from Edmund, Duke of York, King Edward's
fifth son, and through his mother the Lady Anne
Mortimer (heiress and sole surviving child of the
Princess Philippa, and the Earl of March) from
Lionel, Duke of Clarence, third son of that
monarch. His nearest title and only claim to the
crown was derived from his maternal descent,
the male branches of the house of Mortimer
having been, by parliament, declared heirs to

[1] Fabian, p. 456.

Richard the Second,[1] so that by their decease
without issue, both in law and justice, the same
rights and privileges became vested in the
Duchess of York and her descendants.

It is needless to trace the political conflicts
which alternately raised and depressed the opposing parties, or to dwell upon the jealousy and
dissensions, which led to the final overthrow of
the English power in France: suffice it to
say, that from the period of the birth of Margaret Beaufort, the illustrious subject of this
memoir, in 1441, until the birth of her son, the
infant Earl of Richmond in 1456; the vicissitudes and trials of the reigning monarch were
as unceasing as the result was fatal to his re-
putation, and subversive of his power. Henry's
unfitness for government increasing with his years,
and the strength of the Yorkist faction gaining
ground from the martial spirit and gallant conduct of their princely leader, Richard Plantagenet, affairs had at length reached a crisis, that
rendered a decision by the sword inevitable.

With a wise foresight of the misery that must
ensue from civil warfare, and with a politic
desire of averting the calamities that threatened
the divided realm, parliament again interposed,
and enacted that Henry the Sixth should possess
and enjoy the kingdom for the remainder of his

[1] Rot. Parl. v. 484.

life,[1] and that Richard, Duke of York, should be nominated protector of the state,[2] and heir and successor of the reigning sovereign at his demise. Margaret of Anjou, however, was not of a disposition tamely to yield her son's inheritance to her husband's rival. Her ambition spurring the Duke of York to anticipate his honours, the compact was of brief duration, and the war it was intended to prevent, commenced with a spirit of condensed hatred, which ended in scenes of cruelty, and extermination, such as can hardly find a parallel in the history of any nation.

This unnatural feud was not entirely closed until Providence, in compassion to the distracted land, ordained in its own good time, that the sword should be sheathed by the union of these two branches of King Edward's ill-fated house, in the person of the infant prince, who was left with his mother, at Pembroke Castle in Wales, receiving the first rudiments of his education in that land of bards and minstrels, which was laid waste, and almost depopulated by the very monarch, whose offspring we now find striving to exterminate and ruin each other.

These retrospections are full of salutary lessons for those who would strengthen their faith by studying the inscrutable wisdom of Providence. We have here a remarkable instance, how the unlawful

[1] Baker's Chron. p. 194.   [2] Rot. Parl. v. 286.

ambition and evil passions of an individual, apparently the most favoured and prosperous, may
nevertheless fall with heavy retribution on his
whole line of descendants in after generations.
In the unobtrusive path of private life, the mysterious workings of an over-ruling Power are
not so evident ; but the exalted position of
princes renders their lives, as it were, a beacon
to warn those in humbler stations against the same
evil tendencies, only modified, perhaps, in their
case by less extensive powers.   By means of the
rise and fall of kings, history opens to our
contemplation a survey of results so opposed to
the limited views of mankind, that the retributive
justice of God is made apparent even by the most
trivial events.   Unimportant, however, as these
events may appear if considered singly, yet
together, they form so mighty a mass, that, when
cast into those scales in which the good and evil
of life is more impartially weighed than repining
man is apt to allow, the balance vibrates for a
time, until the preponderance of evil, which has
gradually been gaining strength in the lapse of
years, overturns itself, and causes an ascendancy
of the ultimate good which so frequently arises
from apparently overwhelming calamity.

At this juncture of political affairs, among
the most zealous supporters of King Henry the
Sixth, was the persecuted Owen Tudor, and

his son Jasper, Earl of Pembroke, the grandfather and uncle of the young Earl of Richmond;
both of whom bore a most active share in the
dangers, and partook of the reverses of fortune,
which pressed so heavily on the unoffending
monarch.

During the eventful four years, which followed
the open warfare thus ferociously commenced
about the period of the Lady Margaret's widowhood, Henry the Sixth was sometimes a prisoner—
sometimes a conqueror; but never more than
nominally a king. It may, therefore, be well believed that he had little power to protect his
kindred from calamities to which he was himself
subjected, and to which all who were in the re-
motest degree connected with the reigning monarch,
were peculiarly exposed.

The delicacy of the Lady Margaret's position,
as a De Beaufort and a Somerset by birth, was
increased yet more, by the peculiar situation of
her son, the young Henry of Richmond, on account of his double relationship to the House
of Lancaster. In those days of rapine and violence, high-born and wealthy widowhood was
replete with peril. Bereft of her husband when
she was herself but little more than a child,
and called upon to watch over the interests
of her infant son, when her own inexperience
almost equally needed a judicious adviser and

protector; the Lady Margaret's trying situation
was rendered yet more hazardous by her close
alliance with one of the leading factions of that
turbulent era.

In this exigency the Countess of Richmond
entered a second time into the marriage state,
and espoused her near relative Sir Humphrey
Stafford; a step which, whether it resulted
from expediency or attachment, was certainly
a prudent one on her part, as from his near
consanguinity, political bias, high rank, and
powerful connections, the son of the gallant Duke
of Buckingham was peculiarly fitted for the
office of guarding and protecting the widowed
Margaret, his young and wealthy cousin.

Descended from Thomas, Duke of Gloucester,
sixth son of Edward the Third, this younger
branch of the Plantagenets had early espoused,
and always continued firm to the house of Lancaster; and in consideration of these services to
his father, as also to himself, Henry the Sixth,
in the twenty-third of his reign, elevated Humphrey, Earl of Stafford, his near kinsman, to the
dignity of Duke of Buckingham.[1]

The precise year in which the Countess of
Richmond was united to her second husband,
is not known; but sufficient may be gathered
from public records to place it with certainty

[1] Synopsis of the Peerage, vol. i. p. 16.

about the year 1459. In the assignment to her
of certain lands and manors by letters patent
37 Hen. VI., she is styled wife of Henry Stafford, son of Humphrey, Duke of Buckingham,
and late wife of Edmund, Earl of Richmond :[1]
and in the will of the Duke of Buckingham,
dated in 1460, he notices her as his daughter
in the following bequest : " To my son Henry
four hundred marks, to him and to my daughter
Margaret, Countess of Richmond, his wife."[2]
From those and a few other documents, it is
evident that she was married to Sir Humphrey
Stafford at the above mentioned period : for the
valiant nobleman whose will has been quoted, fell
bravely fighting for his sovereign in 1460.

From the testimony, however, of Welsh writers,
it appears that the Lady Margaret continued her
abode in Pembroke Castle ; and Dr. Fuller states
that she there resided for some years,[3] the distracted condition of England affording an uncertain asylum for any connections of the falling
House of Lancaster.

The death of the Duke of York brought matters
at length to a crisis. He was slain at the battle
of Wakefield, in 1461, and the barbarous order
issued by the Queen to place his head in mockery,

[1] Vincent's Corrections of Brooke, p. 87.
[2] Testamenta Vetusta, p. 297.
[3] Fuller's Ch. Hist., Appendix, sec. vi. p. 89.

crowned with a paper diadem over the gates of
York, so exasperated his party, that, concentrating
their forces under the banners of the young Earl
of March, the Duke of York's son and heir,
they so totally discomfited the king's army,
first at Mortimer's Cross, and subsequently at
Towton, that Henry the Sixth was compelled to
fly into Scotland, and Queen Margaret and the
Prince of Wales to take refuge in France.

The flower of the Lancastrian faction were
either slain or afterwards executed without trial,
and the dispersed survivors compelled to seek
safety by exile or concealment. Proceeding
directly to London, the young Duke of York was
proclaimed king by the title of Edward the
Fourth, and crowned at Westminster, towards
the close of the same year, 1461. King Henry
imprudently venturing into England, though in
disguise, was taken prisoner, and committed to
the Tower. The queen, the Prince of Wales,
and their adherents, were attainted by act of
parliament; and Edward of York, to reward
his own partizans, distributed their lands and
possessions amongst such of his followers, as had
served him with the greatest zeal and fidelity.
Owen Tudor, as before mentioned, with many
other distinguished warriors, was beheaded at
Hereford; but Jasper, Earl of Pembroke, eluded
the vigilance of his enemies, and flying from

England was compelled to wander from country to country, enduring the greatest hardships, and for many years suffering the extreme of penury and want.

So long as Henry the Sixth retained even the shadow of royalty, the Countess of Richmond and the young earl remained in comparative tranquillity; but the dethronement of the Lancastrian monarch, and the final ascendancy of the Yorkist faction, by the coronation of King Edward the Fourth, led to a material change in the fortunes of the Lady Margaret and her noble son.

One of the early acts of the new monarch's reign was to attaint the Earl of Richmond,[1] a step probably induced by the active part taken against him by his uncle and guardian, Jasper, Earl of Pembroke, who commanded the Lancastrian forces at Mortimer's Cross, and had ever been the most determined opponent to the claims of the House of York. King Edward, by letters patent, stripped the young Henry Tudor of his territorial possessions, and bestowed them on his own brother George, Duke of Clarence; but he did not grant him the dignity of Earl of Richmond, nor did the royal duke ever assume that title.[2]

[1] Rot. Parl. 1. Edw. IV. p. 2., m. 19 and 21.

[2] Report on the Dignity of the Peerage, p. 130.

The Lady Margaret appears to have been treated more favourably, as by the act of restitution, 1 Ed. IV. 1461, the rights of the Countess of Richmond in lands which she held in dower, of Edmund, late Earl of Richmond, were saved to her, as well as all lands which descended to her from her father John, late Duke of Somerset.[1]

In a similar act to that just cited, in 1464, the interests of Sir Henry Stafford, Knight, and Margaret, his wife, Countess of Richmond in the same lands are allowed,[2] and again the same year her rights are confirmed by another act of parliament.[3] Whether this leniency arose from her recent alliance with so influential and powerful a family as that of Stafford, or whether the king determined to wreak his vengeance on Jasper Tudor, by attainting and impoverishing his nephew, must remain a mere matter of speculation; the probable inference is, that revenge actuated his conduct to the son, and policy that to the mother. Few, indeed, understood the art of acquiring popular favour so well as Edward the Fourth: not only did he pay marked attention to those who had served him in the most critical time; but he wisely endeavoured to attach to his interest as many as could be gained by acts of conciliation from the opposite party.[4] Notwith-

[1] Rot. Parl. v. 471.   [2] Ibid. v. 523.   [3] Ibid. v. 285.
[4] Paston Letters. vol. i. p. 239.

standing the grace, however, which extended and
was continued to the Countess of Richmond; her
near connection with the deposed monarch, and
her direct descent from John of Gaunt, rendered
both herself and her son objects of jealous watchfulness to King Edward. Though far removed
from the cabals and intrigues of the Court, they
were residents in the abode of his bitterest
enemy, the outlawed Earl of Pembroke; whose
rich possessions were too important to be left in
abeyance when so many who had fought for the
House of York were but poorly and insufficiently
rewarded.

Foremost in the number of these was Sir William Herbert, Lord of Ragland, in Monmouth-
shire, who for his manifold services, and eminent
merits, obtained a grant to him and his heirs of
the Castle, town and lordship of Pembroke, with
all its members, and appurtenances. Thither he
was forthwith ordered to remove with his family,
in consequence of the noble relatives of the attainted Jasper Tudor having been committed to
his custody, so that from this time the sojourn
of the Lady Margaret and her son in Wales,
was not by choice as a voluntary home, but by
sufferance, and in what might almost be viewed
(especially as regards the latter) in the light of state
prisoners; in confirmation of which it is on record
that the young Earl of Richmond, at a later

period of his life, informed Philip Comines, the Flemish historian,[1] that he had been in prison, or under strict command, from five years old. Now this was his age at the historical era under consideration, and in some respects the change was as advantageous as it must have been pleasing to his youthful fancy. Sir William Herbert's family, consisting of four sons and six daughters, afforded him companions in his own sphere of life, and gave him opportunities to acquire accomplishments and exercises, that would have been wholly unattainable on account of the retired habits which had been forced on the Countess of Richmond by the distracted state of the land.

But these advantages were more than counterbalanced in the estimation of his anxious parent, by the perilous situation in which the attainder of himself and the heads of his family had placed her only child. She viewed with misgiving and alarm the rigour exercised against the line of Lancaster. She felt that his tender years were his only protection, and that he was left unmolested in Pembroke Castle, merely as a hostage for his outlawed kindred. The Lady Margaret had a greatness of soul, that could sustain any personal evil, and endure with equanimity the extremes of good or bad fortune; because her thoughts were unceasingly fixed on a better state

[1] Philip de Comines, v. p. 514.

of existence, so that she was neither elated with
prosperity, nor could be wholly subdued by ad-.
versity.[1] But as regards her son her emotions
were strong, and her anxiety painfully acute. He
had been the infant sharer of her affliction, he
was the chief object of her solicitude, and for
him she entertained the most fervent affection :
all, therefore, that regarded his present and possibly his future career, excited her feelings most
powerfully ; and the ardour with which she devoted herself to his interests, to guarding his
childish days from evil, and striving to invigorate
his dawning intellect against sudden reverses or
unlooked-for dangers, was never obliterated from
his mind. Its remembrance indeed was cherished
to his latest years, with a warmth of feeling—
a respectful deference, well merited from the
anxiety and forethought exercised by the young
Countess of Richmond, the admired heiress of
Somerset, in the prime of her youth and beauty,
from a tender desire to guard and protect the
offspring of her early love.

The tendency of the precepts so strongly
impressed on the ductile mind of his infancy
was soon shown in the opening character of the
young Earl. He grew up sad, serious, and circum-
spect ; full of thought, and secret observation ;
peaceable in disposition, just and merciful in

[1] Fisher's Funeral Sermon, p. 29.

action. From the old Flemish historians,[1] and his biographer Lord Bacon,[2] it further appears, that " He was fair and well spoken, with singular sweetness and blandishment of words, rather studious than learned, with a devotional cast of countenance ; for he was marvellously religious both in affection and observance."

These were the characteristics developed in the child whom Sir William Herbert and his family found resident with his mother, in their newly allotted domain of Pembroke Castle. He appears to have excited no common degree of interest in the hearts of his guardians, and to have continued to win upon their love and affection, as he advanced in years, as it is asserted, that by the Lady Herbert he was well and carefully educated,[3] and that Sir William desired to see him wedded to his favourite daughter Maud.[4] So tranquilly, indeed, did the lives of both families glide on, in their secluded abode, that a betrothment as youthful as that of the Lady Margaret with Edmund Tudor, might possibly have been the result, had not a counter-revolution again rent asunder the ties of domestic comfort, and once more plunged the land into all the horrors of civil war.

[1] Philip de Comines, Froissart, and Lobineau.
[2] Bacon's Hen. VII., p. 244, 246, and 233.
[3] Polydore Virgil, 522, f. 10.   [4] Dugdale, ii. p. 239.

In the eighth year of King Edward's reign, the indefatigable and zealous Jasper Tudor having by unceasing efforts collected a small body of men, landed in North Wales, where he was soon joined by his kindred. He was, however, speedily opposed by Sir William Herbert, who compelling him, by the most determined and continued defeat, again to fly the realm; the king, after having bestowed on this faithful adherent fresh honours, completed the measure of his favours, by advancing him to the title of Earl of Pembroke, which was then in the Crown, by the attainder of his brave opponent.

But the popularity of the gallant monarch had long been on the wane. Addicted wholly to pleasure, and devoting his days to frivolous dissipation, and indolent enjoyment, Edward the Fourth gave, in time of peace, full opportunity for his enemies to rally their strength, and prepare for renewed warfare. Having mortally offended the potent Earl of Warwick, and many other of the chief leaders of his party, by imprudently marrying the beautiful widow of a Lancastrian noble; conspiracies and cabals, gave indication of the approaching storm which had long been gathering on the political horizon.

In the year 1468, open rebellion was declared in the north; the new Earl of Pembroke and his brother Sir Richard Herbert, assembled a con-

siderable body of the Welsh to oppose the insurrection; but their party being vanquished at
Banbury with great loss, the two brothers, after
performing prodigies of valour,[1] were taken prisoners and beheaded at Northampton. The earl
by his last testament repeated the desire so long
indulged, that his daughter Maud should marry
the Lord Henry of Richmond.[2]

The Lancastrian leaders having returned from
France, with a powerful force, headed by the
Earl of Warwick; Edward the Fourth, after brief
but vigorous resistance, was compelled to flee the
country, and abdicate the throne. The unfortunate Henry the Sixth was taken from the
Tower, where he had been imprisoned nearly
nine years, and on the 6th October, 1470, with
great pomp was restored to his kingdom, and reinstated in his authority as sovereign of the realm.

Among the number of the exiled nobility who
accompanied the Earl of Warwick, was Jasper
Tudor: landing safely in the west with a determined band, he forthwith proceeded into Wales,
to visit his territory and increase his force. There
he found the Countess of Richmond, and his
orphan nephew, resident in the custody of the
widow of the brave and recently ennobled Earl
of Pembroke.[3]

---

[1] Anglorum Speculum, 966. [2] Dugdale's Baron. ii. p. 241.
[3] Cotton MS. Dom. xviii. f. 135.

Though strictly watched, and considered in the light of a captive, the youthful Earl had been most courteously treated, and honourably brought up, by the Lady Herbert. Andreas Scott, a priest of Oxford, is stated to have been his preceptor, and Henry's contemporary biographer (before alluded to) in recording this fact,[1] mentions also the eulogiums bestowed by him on his great capacity, and aptitude for study.

Nevertheless, as he was now fourteen years of age, and as his close imprisonment had deprived him of many advantages suitable to his high estate, his uncle immediately took him from Wales, and carried him to London, where, after being presented to King Henry the Sixth, he was placed as a scholar at Eton ;[1] a college founded by that pious monarch in his more prosperous days. This singularly amiable prince, fitted by his praise-worthy qualities to shine in private life, though unhappily for himself and his kindred, not possessing the talent suited to rule over a contested and disunited realm, was attending a feast at his munificent foundation of Eton, shortly after Henry of Richmond had been placed there. Chancing accidentally to cast his eyes on him, he steadfastly regarded him for a time, and then turning to the assembled nobles, he exclaimed, as it would seem prophetically, " This

[1] Sandford's Geneal. vi. ch. 10.

is the lad who shall possess that for which we now strive."[1]

K. *Henry.*—" My Lord of Somerset what youth is that
Of whom you seem to have so tender care ?"
  Som.—" My liege, it is young Henry, Earl of Richmond."
  K.*Henry.*—"Come hither, England's hope. If secret powers
Suggest but truth to my divining thoughts,
This pretty lad will prove our country's bliss.
His looks are full of peaceful majesty ;
His head by nature fram'd to wear a crown,
His hand to wield a sceptre ; and himself
Likely, in time, to bless a regal throne.
Make much of him, my lords ; for this is he,
Must help you more, than you are hurt by me."
                              Henry VI. Scene vi, Act iv.

This prognostication, thus beautifully rendered by the immortal Shakspeare, had a strong influence on Richmond's after-life. It early fixed the eyes of the court upon him, and proves also the light in which he was considered from his boyhood by the Lancastrian leaders. In all the conflicts that ensued, both for the regency and the throne, his mother's family, the powerful Somersets, had enlisted themselves as interested parties ; and Henry the Sixth may probably have had it in view to nominate Richmond as his successor, in the event of his own son's death without issue : for the Lady Margaret's offspring in that case would have been his nearest heir in descent from

[1] Bacon's Hen. VII., p. 247.

John of Gaunt. Whatever may have been the
cause of the seemingly prophetic ejaculation, it
sufficiently accounts for the jealousy felt by the
Yorkists towards the young Earl, and for the persecutions he was quickly to endure at their hands.

During the brief triumph of the Lancastrian
party by the liberation of Henry the Sixth, his
maternal brother Jasper Tudor, was reinstated in
his Earldom, and fully restored to all his honours
and possessions ; but it was a very temporary enjoyment. A few months enabled Edward the
Fourth to collect a sufficient body of foreign
mercenaries, and to land privately at Ravenspur,
in Yorkshire, and though prudently avoiding the
hazard of a battle, he made himself so formidable
to his opponents as he advanced towards the
metropolis, that Jasper Tudor felt the necessity
of withdrawing the young Earl, his nephew, from
Eton, and sending him again for greater security
to Wales; the Lady Margaret, his mother, having
continued to sojourn there until more tranquil
times enabled her to remove elsewhere with
safety.

The signal defeat of the Lancastrians at the
battle of Barnet, speedily laid prostrate the short-
lived hopes of the Red Rose faction, which were
wholly crushed by the result of the conflict at
Tewksbury, and the deaths which immediately
followed, first of the Prince of Wales, and then

of his ill-fated and care-worn parent ; for having been again taken prisoner, and again deposed and committed to the Tower, he died there suddenly in the year 1471, leaving his rival Edward the Fourth in quiet possession of the throne.*

The demise of these two princes placed the Countess of Richmond and the young Earl, in a very different position from that, which they had hitherto held.

By the death of Edward, Prince of Wales, Henry the Sixth's only child, the royal family of the Lancastrian line had become extinct ; and the offspring of the Lady Margaret, the representative and heiress of the eldest surviving male

* The MS. recently published by the Camden Society, from the original in the British Museum (Harl. MSS. 543, f. 3,) satisfactorily controverts the long accredited tale, that Edward, Prince of Wales, was assassinated in cold blood after the battle of Tewksbury, by the heads of the House of York ; and that Henry the Sixth was inhumanly murdered in the Tower, by the Duke of Gloucester, afterwards Richard the Third. At page 30 of the above cited MS., the author says, " Edward called Prince, was taken fleinge to towne-wards, and slayne in the field." And in recording the death of Henry the Sixth, p. 38, he asserts that of pure displeasure and melancholy he died the xxiij day of the month of May." A fact perfectly reconcileable with the debilitated state to which long illness, constitutional infirmities, and undue exertion had reduced the unhappy monarch. —See " The historie of the arrival of King Edward the Fourth in England, and the finall recoverye of his kingdomes from Henry the Sixth."

branch of John of Gaunt's descendants, became,
in the estimation of the vanquished faction, not
merely the head of their almost exterminated
race, but also the next heir to the throne, and
lawful inheritor of the deceased monarch's possessions. Henry of Richmond, however, was
considered to have derived but an imperfect title
to the crown from his illustrious mother, in consequence of the illegitimate connection which stig-
matised her descent from the House of Lancaster. " A disabling brand," as justly observed by
a modern author, "in that day of proud nobility."[1] It is true the De Beauforts had been
legitimated by act of parliament, February 1397,
and enabled to enjoy all lands and hereditary
seignories ; but the charter, it was generally considered, conferred on them no pretension to
the crown, there being a special exception
with respect to the royal dignity. It would appear, however, from recent discoveries that the
Lady Margaret and her illustrious son possessed higher claim to the throne than has
hitherto been surmised; or than they probably
themselves believed. In the original letters
patent obtained by the Duke of Lancaster, from
Richard the Second, 1397,[2] there is neither re-
servation nor exception whatsoever. The De

[1] Sharon Turner, vol. iii. p. 239.
[2] Rot. Parl. 20 Rich. II. vol. iii. p. 343.

Beauforts were to be " admitted to all honours and all dignities."

At the time, however, when this legitimacy was thus amicably established, the children of John of Gaunt appeared far removed from all prospect of inheriting the crown ; but Henry the Fourth having usurped it, from Richard the Second, and possession being secured to him by act of parliament, in defiance of the hereditary claims of elder branches of Edward the Third's family; the De Beauforts as the nearest kindred of the reigning sovereign, were placed in a far different position. Whether actuated by jealousy of his recently acknowledged brothers, or whether as a usurper himself, he was keenly alive to the possibility of rivalship in them, need not here be discussed, and would, indeed, be at best a mere opinion : it is only the result of his conduct that is important, since his jealous precautions gave rise to the belief that the Somersets, who acted so conspicuous a part during the reigns of the Lancastrian monarchs, were excluded from all heirship or succession to the throne.

The Duke of Somerset, on Henry's accession, applied to him to exemplify and confirm the act of legitimation granted by his predecessor. He acceded, but it would seem not without effecting a most material change in the original document ;[1]

[1] Excerpta Historica, 152.

for it appears that in the reign of Henry the
Fourth, after the words all "honours and dignities,"
an interlineation of the words, "except to the
royal dignity," was added to the enrolment on the
Patent Rolls;[1] in a somewhat different hand, and
altogether a different coloured ink.   This clause
is presumed to have been inserted by that monarch
in his exemplification to the Earl of Somerset, in
1407, just ten years after the original grant, an
interval of time sufficiently small to account for
the universally received opinion that the De
Beauforts were from the first excluded from all
claims to the English throne.   This most singular
and curious discovery shows that Henry of Richmond was indeed the lineal heir of John of Gaunt,
and the representative, as he asserted, of the
House of Lancaster.[2]

But the fearful era which marked the wars of the
Roses, was one in which the sword triumphed
over law and justice, no right was acknowledged,
but that of power — no claim admitted, but by
force of arms.   The Lady Margaret and her son
were generally believed to be excluded from all
pretension to the throne; but even had their
claim been allowed, the priority of those of York
was incontestable.   Nevertheless the near relationship of Edmund Tudor to the deposed

[1] See Appendix B.
[2] Privy Purse Expences of Elizabeth of York, p. 61.

monarch, coupled with the consanguinity of Margaret of Lancaster to the fallen House, made her offspring an object of jealous apprehension, to the White Rose faction, and of hopeful expectation to its rival.

After the defeat of his party at Tewksbury, Jasper Tudor took refuge in his almost impregnable castle at Pembroke, in which, for equal security, his nephew and the Countess his mother were still sojourning. Assured that as long as any of King Henry's kindred lived, and were at liberty, he should never be free from plots against his life and throne, Edward the Fourth endeavoured to entrap the cautious Earl, when he heard of his escape after the great overthrow of his party; but Jasper eluded his vigilance, and took summary vengeance on the treachery of the spies who were sent to dispatch him.

Finding, however, that the king had re-instated the son and heir of Sir William Herbert in the earldom of Pembroke, he foresaw that strong measures would be speedily adopted for his capture. He resolved, therefore, to be prepared for defence; nor were his precautions unneeded, for he was besieged in his fortress by Morgan ap Thomas, a zealous friend and partisan of the House of York, by whom he was so closely pressed, that he must soon have surrendered, had not David ap Thomas, another brother, who had em-

braced the Lancastrian cause, come promptly and
opportunely to his assistance.   This chieftain,
aware that King Edward's object was to prevent
the illustrious inmates escaping out of the country,
hastily collected a strong body of ill-armed, but
resolute Welsh, who falling unexpectedly on the
besiegers, compelled them to retire; and in the
confusion which ensued, their brave deliverer following up his victory, conveyed the Countess of
Richmond with her son, and Jasper Tudor, to
Tenby, from whence they immediately embarked
and sailed for the coast of France ; the Earl
of Pembroke having not long before been
most courteously received by Louis the Eleventh,
when, with other of the exiled noblesse, he had
rallied round the standard of the unfortunate
Margaret of Anjou and Prince Edward of Lancaster, prior to their last visit to England.

But their trials were only slightly diminished,
when the fugitives escaped from their enemies.
The elements appeared to conspire against them,[1]
for scarcely had they put to sea, when an awful storm
arose, which not only threatened their destruction, but frustrated all their plans, as regarded
landing in France.   The wind being contrary, and
its violence extreme, they were driven far out of
their course, and, after having been placed in imminent peril, and preserved by little less than a
miracle, they were at length cast upon the shores

of Brittany. They gained St. Maloes with some
difficulty, and were resting there to recruit their
exhausted energies, when fresh evil was at hand,
to damp their small stock of remaining courage ;
for information having been forwarded to Francis,
the reigning Duke of that state, he forthwith ordered them to be arrested, and conveyed as prisoners to the castle of Vannes.

This breach of hospitality has been ascribed to
various causes, though by none can it be justified.
The most probable motive for their capture
seems to have been the advantage that was likely
to result to Duke Francis, from their detention as
hostages to restrain within bounds the ambition
of the English Monarch, and to reap the full benefit which must accrue to the Duchy, from a secure alliance with England, in case of a rupture
between himself and the French King. The prediction of Henry the Sixth, it seems, had reached
his ears, and that he had heard, from others, that
Richmond would reign. Subsequent events prove
the policy of the Duke's foresight, though it did
not palliate his ungenerous conduct in arresting
the unfortunate shipwrecked party ; for he was enabled to keep the English completely under sub-
jection so long as the head of the Lancastrian
faction remained at his disposal, and no less to
trifle with the French King,[1] who, from his own
motives, strove to obtain possession of a rival so

dreaded by Edward the Fourth. That King was indeed outrageous, when he heard of the flight of the noble party,[1] and was only calmed by learning they were prisoners, with his ally, the Duke of Brittany, instead of exiles at the court of a Monarch, whose actions were so opposed to his professions, as those of Louis the Eleventh. At any sacrifice, however, would Edward of York have ransomed them into his own power ; he sent costly presents to Francis, and offered him great rewards for their delivery ; but the wary Duke feigned that he could not, in honour, abandon those whom calamity had cast on his protection. He pledged himself, however, for their safe custody, and engaged to keep so unceasing a watch over their actions, that King Edward could, by no possibility, be endangered, either in his person or throne.

With this promise, the Monarch was compelled to rest satisfied, and the young Henry Tudor[2] was once more closely imprisoned. His personal attendants were withdrawn and dismissed shortly after to their homes, native Bretons being appointed by Duke Francis in their stead ; and, to increase the severity exercised towards him, he was also separated from his uncle Jasper Tudor, who was sent to a distant fortress, and there guarded with extreme vigilance.[3] The Castle of Vannes, where

[1] Baker's Chron. p. 215.　　　[2] Philip de Comines, 1, 514.
[3] Lobineau's Hist. Brotagne, 1, p. 751.

the Earl continued, was strictly watched within,
and surrounded without by a guard of soldiers,[1] so that, though treated with the courtesy
befitting their elevated rank, the Lord of Pembroke, and his noble nephew, were considered as
state prisoners, and continued to be viewed as
such for a length of time.

The youthful Earl of Richmond was now about
fifteen years of age, and, even from his birth, can
scarcely be said to have enjoyed the blessings of
liberty.   Hitherto, however, he had benefited by
the wise counsel, and been made happy by the
society of his mother; but at this period, the
sorrows of the Lady Margaret and her son were
heightened by the pang of separation.

The annals of the Duchy of Brittany make no
mention of the Countess, when treating of circumstances connected with the imprisonment of the
Earl of Pembroke or the young Henry of Richmond.[2]   Tradition asserts, that she accompanied
them in their perilous voyage ;[3] but the probability
is, that she proceeded no further than Tenby; the
Earl of Pembroke having proposed, before they
were besieged by Morgan ap Thomas, that his

[1] Froissart.

[2] Buck, p. 16.

[3] Rymer, speaking of after events in her life, says " Margaret, mother to the Earl of Richmond who was a refugee in
Bretagne," vol. ii. p. 2.

nephew should flee with him to France for security ; his grandmother, Katherine of Valois (wife
of Owen ap Tudor) having been aunt to the
reigning monarch. The Lady Margaret, however,
opposed the scheme, and suggested their trusting
to the many strongholds in Wales, but Jasper
knew that Richmond's life would be sought, and
subsequent events made his alarmed parent gladly
consent to his seeking safety by flight ; whether,
therefore, she accompanied them to Brittany, and
was compelled to return to England, when his
retinue were dismissed, and his uncle removed to
another fortress, or whether she voluntarily resigned her child to the protection of Jasper Tudor,
under the impression that her presence might em-
barrass their future efforts at escape, is not known.
As, however, frequent allusions are made to the
hardships which she endured for the sake of her
son, it may confidently be inferred that the Lady
Margaret had to struggle with severe trials, before
she could establish herself in any part of her inheritance, and that the personal sufferings of both
parent and child were greatly aggravated by a premature and hopeless separation.

The exterminating and disastrous wars which,
with little intermission, had marked ·the epoch
from the marriage of Margaret Beaufort with Edmund Tudor to the period of their son's imprisonment in the Castle of Vannes, was no less

fraught with misery to England than with desolation to the kindred of both their illustrious
families. The Duchess of Somerset, her mother,
was dead, and slept by the side of her valiant husband, at Wimborne Minster; Leo, Lord Welles,
the Lady Margaret's father-in-law, was killed at the
battle of Towton; that of St. Alban's numbered
her uncle, the Duke of Somerset, amongst its slain;
Mortimer's Cross terminated the career of Owen
ap Tudor, and the chief of her son's Welsh connections; while Northampton was rendered memorable, by the fall of the Duke of Buckingham, the
gallant father of her present husband. Of the
many noble and distinguished relatives who had
hailed the descendant of John of Gaunt, as the
bride of the King's brother, little more than ten
years previously, scarcely one now remained, when
the Countess of Richmond returned to the home
of her birth, and sought out the remnant of those
ties of kindred, the greater portion of which was
so painfully and irrevocably broken.

Fearful, indeed, had been the changes, both political and domestic, during her seclusion in Wales.
King Henry the Sixth, after being four times a
prisoner, and twice deprived of his kingdom, slept
with his forefathers, as did his ill-fated and princely
son. Queen Margaret of Anjou, ransomed by
her father from imprisonment, was a widow, and
childless, a broken-hearted exile in her native land.

The bitterest enemies of their race wielded the sceptre of England; the devoted friends of their house were outcasts and wanderers. Edward of York, after having been himself a prisoner, compelled to fly the country, deprived of his crown, and proclaimed an usurper and traitor by his own brother, the Duke of Clarence, and his once firm friend the Earl of Warwick, was seated, more firmly than before, on the throne of his ancestors; with the unassuming, Lady Margaret, and her exiled child, as his only rivals, and probable opponents.

The blood royal of England, indeed, was nearly extinguished, and the flower of its nobility had perished in the field, or on the scaffold. The hereditary, and rich provinces in France, which had belonged to the Kings of England, were irrecoverably lost. Ireland was a wilderness,—the national wealth was exhausted—and the people oppressed with evils of every kind, were sunk in the depths of ignorance and misery.[1] Darkness might truly be said to overshadow the land. Parents had fought against their children; fathers had fallen by the hands of their sons; brothers betrayed each other into the power of the enemy, and every tie, human and divine, was severed and disregarded. No wonder that literature did not advance, or that the kingdom was without knowledge. No wonder

[1] Camden's Britt. vol. 2, p. 916.

that a veil has been tacitly drawn over the era that
marks the wars of the Roses ; an era that reduced
the glories of our once favoured isle, to the
ferocious barbarity of her primitive and savage
state; an era that made her chieftains executioners
—her people the victims of penury and want.

A fearful picture this of the misery which civil
war entails on countless multitudes. Would that
in this matter we could believe the prejudices
of party spirit had multiplied the extent of the
evil, or the pen of romance under the garb of
history, transformed, by its embellishment, simple
truth to almost incredible fiction; but one of the
most indefatigable writers of the present age[1] has
only confirmed by his valuable researches, and
plain unvarnished statement, the harrowing scenes
impressed upon the youthful mind for centuries
past by the Bard of Avon.[2]

Leaving then Edward the Fourth in tranquil
possession of a throne which was so fiercely contested and so dearly purchased, it will be refreshing to pass from public to private life; and consider a little more in detail, that domestic career
of the Countess of Richmond from which attention
has been somewhat too largely withdrawn by the
review of political events.

With that discretion which she so frequently

[1] Sharon Turner, vol. iii, pp. 299—373.
[2] Henry vi. act ii. scene v.

displayed in avoiding danger by precautionary measures, and which, as before observed, so strongly marked her character, the Lady Margaret shunned all contact with her enemies, by leading a life of the strictest privacy, in the most secluded places of her inheritance. A great part of her possessions and those of her son, had been wrested from them during their abode in Wales, or had passed into other hands in that turbulent and uncertain period. Baynard's Castle had been held by the house of York from the time of her first husband's decease, and was now the palace of the king and the occasional residence of his mother Cicely, Duchess of York ; and the county of Richmondshire, with its castle and rich domains, had been taken from the exiled Earl, and bestowed by the reigning monarch, first upon his brother the Duke of Clarence,[1] and after his death, upon Richard of Gloucester.[2] Notwithstanding these changes, and many which bore more immediately on her own individual patrimony, her manorial rights, and rich lands in various counties were so valuable, and yielded, as may be judged from her immense wealth in after years, so large a revenue, that it may reasonably be inferred that the Lady Margaret, with her prudent foresight, and strong maternal feelings, judiciously devoted this period of her life to

[1] Rot. Pat. 11 Ed. IV. pars 2. m. 19 and 21.
[2] Rot. Pat. 18 Ed. IV. pars 1. m. 22.

provident measures for the endowment of her
now portionless child ; King Edward, on his
restoration, having confiscated the lands and
goods of all persons that had taken part against
him, or fled from the arm of the law.[1]

She seems to have dwelt for some time at Tor-
rington, in Devonshire ; for it is on record that the
manse being far removed from the church, she
bestowed on the minister there and his successors, her manor-house and lands appertaining
to it which were situated close to the sacred
edifice.[2]

By her charities at Wimborne, Hatfield, and
Fordham, she probably sojourned also at each of
these places occasionally; but her chief residence
was Collyweston[3] in Northamptonshire, where she
erected a stately mansion, on the site of one commenced by Lord Cromwell, lord treasurer to
Henry the Sixth.[4] The property on which it stood
was important[5] by reason of the slate quarries adjoining; and the spirit of benevolence which was so
inherent in her nature, had here ample scope for
its exercise, in mitigating the sufferings of the
hard-working poor, who laboured at the building
she was erecting, or wrought in the adjacent

[1] Baker's Chron. p. 213.　　[2] Magna Brit. p. 489.
[3] Leland's Itin. vol. i. p. 23.
[4] Leland's Itin. vol. vi. p. 28.
[5] Camden's Brit. vol. i. p. 526.

mines. Charity indeed appears to have been the
mainspring of her every thought and action. It
was this charity that led her to shun the path of
discord, and strive for that of peace ; to endure
evil from her enemies with meekness and patience,
and to submit to the trials of her allotted path
with cheerfulness, humility, and fortitude.

Though practising in the overstrained spirit
of the faith in which she had been nurtured, the
most rigid mortification, and voluntarily enduring
the most painful self-discipline, she was always
mindful of the sufferings of others. Her deep
sense of religion has justly been the theme
of eulogium to all who have recorded her virtues,
and whilst she austerely performed the rites
appointed by the papal church, she so uni-
formly blended with these the steady practice of
every moral duty, that her actions excite the
admiration of the present generation, as they did
that of the far distant, and unenlightened period
in which she flourished. [1]

In the performance of her conjugal and maternal
duties, she has been justly held up as a bright example to her sex. Nevertheless every earthly feeling was chastened by the higher claims due to her
Maker. It was her habit to rise at five, and she
invariably passed the time till ten—the dinner-time
of that period—in deep meditation and prayer.
The remainder of the day was given to the exercise

of every virtue that could adorn with christian grace
her exalted rank. Wherever was her abiding place,
blessings followed the steps of the illustrious Margaret.   Thus disposed to religion and charity,
she was peculiarly qualified for the secluded life
which she had been called upon to lead, first
by necessity, and now by choice, while sorrowing
in secret for her son's exile. Happily her studious habits rendered her retirement anything but
irksome, while it induced the cultivation of talents,
the result of which has added to her fame by
ranking her amongst the earliest of England's
female authors, and which led to her proving
in more peaceful days, the patron of able contemporaries, and one of the greatest benefactors to learning, either of her own or of succeeding ages.

At what precise period the Lady Margaret commenced the works that have been handed down to
posterity is uncertain, but probably the task that
devolved on her of superintending the education of
her son, the young Henry of Richmond, during their
lengthened sojourn in Wales, first led her to devote
a portion of each day to translating from French
into English, books of scholastic divinity.

This laborious task would scarcely perhaps be
admitted as a claim to authorship in these favoured
times, when vocabularies and lexicons are abundant,
and books of reference easy of access and cheaply

more especially at so dark an era as the close of the
fifteenth century, the merit of translation with exact-
ness, and the positive toil and talent requisite for the
employment, render these labours one of the most
interesting and remarkable features in her history.
That these extremely rare and curious MSS., the
work of the Countess of Richmond, were the produce of the prime and vigour of her days, seems
probable, from their being amongst the earliest
and most valuable specimens extant of English
typography; and that she was eminent for studious
habits, and remarkable for close application to
books during the time of her second marriage, is
shown by the will of her husband's mother, the
Duchess Dowager of Buckingham, who bequeathed
her in her last testament the following legacy : —

"To my daughter of Richmond, a book of
English, called ' Legenda Sanctorum,' being a
legend of saints:—A book of French, called
' Lucun;' another book in French of the Epistles
and Gospels, and a primmer with clasps of silver
gilt, covered with purple velvet." [1]—A considerable
legacy this, for that age, both as regards the rarity
and intrinsic worth of the bequest.

On the taking of Paris about fifty years
previous, the Duke of Bedford sent in triumph
to England the royal library of France, [2] which,
although it consisted of only 800 volumes, was

[1] Testamenta Vetusta, p. 357.   [2] Life of Caxton, p. 15.

valued at 2,300*l.*, an enormous sum at that
period. These works, which were of course all
in MSS., afterwards formed the foundation of
the library which was bestowed by Humphery,
Duke of Gloucester, on the University of Oxford
in the year 1440, when, out of 600 volumes,
120 alone, we are told, were valued at more
than 1000*l.* of the money of that day.

These facts, though not immediately connected
with the Lady Margaret's history, are inserted to
strengthen her claim to be classed amongst those
literary female characters, whose writings and skill
in languages, have ranked them amongst the
learned of the land. The bequest of the Duchess
of Buckingham shows the nature of the books
that were alone likely to be attainable by her
daughter-in-law, and the scarcity and great
cost of such works as were needful to aid her
in the task of translation, is apparent from the
great value and limited extent of public and royal
libraries at the time that Margaret of Lancaster
headed the list of the learned women of England.
As regards choice of language, and purity of
diction, her productions are deservedly held high
in estimation, as standard specimens of the style
of that age; for the merits of a work should be
estimated by the difficulties to be surmounted in
its accomplishment at the time, and not merely by

H

comparison with similar undertakings at a later period.

Among the works which were the result of the Lady Margaret's studious hours, (or rather such as have been preserved to the present day,) stands conspicuous: "The Mirroure of Golde for the Sinfull Soule," previously translated at Paris, from a Latin work, entitled "Speculum Aureum Peccatorum," and subsequently, rendered, by her, from French into English.

The preface of this exceedingly rare, and curious book, (of which a very fine copy is preserved in the valuable Biblical library of His Royal Highness the Duke of Sussex,) makes us acquainted with the nature of its contents, which are as follows: "For to know the order and maner how to procede in this lytell boke, it is to know it shall be divided in seven chapitoures after the seven dayes of the weeke, To thentent that the synfull soule, soyled and defouled by synne, maye, in every chapitoure, have a new mirroure, wherein he may beholde and consider the face of his soule."

The table of these chapters is as follows:

"Firste — Of the filthines and miserie of man.

"Seconde— Of synnes in generalle, and of their effectes.

" Thyrde — Howe they ought hastily, with all diligence to do penance.

" Fourthe. — Howe they ought to flee the worlde.

" Fyfthe. —'Of the false riches, and vayne honours of the worlde.

" Sixth—Howe they ought to dred deth.

" Seventh—Of the joyes of Paradyse, and of the paynes of Hell !"[1]

The other chief production of the Lady Margaret's pen, which has escaped the ravages of time, is " The imitation and following of the blessed life of our most merciful Saviour Christ ;" being a translation from French into English, of the fourth book of Dr. John Gersen's (or Kempis's) treatise, " De imitatione Christi."

In Dr. Fuller's Church History, there is also a notice relative to some prayers published some years after by her command ; and the nature of her devout occupations, and literary habits, would warrant the inference, that these too were her own composition.

While thus pursuing in comparative tranquillity, a career, alike honourable to herself and beneficial to those around her, the young Henry Tudor, her son, divested of his inheritance, and deprived of his liberty, was passing the prime of his life in hopeless exile, debarred from the indulgence of those warm affec-

---

[1] Extracted from the copy at Kensington Palace.

tions, and denied all those active enjoyments
which gladden the heart of youth. The captive
Richmond had early been tutored by his exemplary parent to place his trust in Heaven, and to
submit with patient endurance to present evils,
under the firm belief, that in God's own good
time, he would surely work out his wise though
hidden purpose.

His unrepining submission to the strict imprisonment, rigorously enforced by the Duke of
Brittany, gradually created a feeling of interest
and compassion in those who were charged with
his custody.

His misfortunes, and the romance of his life,
gained him many friends connected with the
court, and at length excited the especial commiseration of the Duke's consort, the noble-minded
Margaret of Brittany, daughter of the celebrated
Gaston de Foix. Edward the Fourth, full of
apprehension of the danger that might ensue to
his family, so long as this last scion of the Red
Rose survived, had, from the first date of his imprisonment, continued to preserve unshaken the
league with his ally by means of large sums of
money, and most costly presents to Francis, and
his chief ministers.

Until Henry of Richmond had attained his
twentieth year, the vigilance pledged by the Duke
had been strictly observed ; but at this period, a

strong party began to form in his favour, both in
the courts of Brittany and France. The peculiar
sweetness of manner and address with which by
nature he was gifted, enabled the attainted Earl
to improve this feeling. Philip de Comines,
who knew him well, testifies that he was perfect
in that courtly breeding, which so conciliates
favour in princes who are ready of access, and
plausible in speech. He had become master of
the French language during his exile, and though
in consequence of his long imprisonment, and
the trials which had saddened his early life, he
was singularly cautious and timid, he had nevertheless gained from the same school of adversity,
a wisdom that enabled him to profit by any
favouring circumstance that might lead to more
prosperous days.

The English monarch, who attentively watched
every change of opinion in foreign and domestic
policy, soon became sensible that his rival was
engaging the attention of many powerful princes,[1]
and strengthening his interest in every possible
way, through the co-operation of the exiled adherents of the Lancastrian family, who had
sought shelter in most of the principal kingdoms
in Europe.

Finding that neither money would purchase the
ransom of his victim, nor bribes effect his delivery

[1] Baker's Chron. p. 215.

into his hands, the wary monarch resolved on changing his line of conduct, and trying to gain by underhand dealing, that compliance from the Duke Francis, which open treaty and earnest solicitation had failed to win. He accordingly dispatched ambassadors to his ally, to sue for the release of the exiled Earl, under the plea of desiring to cement the long protracted disputes of the two opposing parties, by means of the union of Henry Tudor with the princess Elizabeth, his eldest daughter.[1] This subtle device succeeded. The Duke of Brittany, deceived by the eloquent and persuasive address of Dr. Stillington, then chancellor, and Bishop of Bath and Wells, delivered the Earl into his care, sending him with a strong guard to St. Maloes, to prevent his escape into France.

But the son of the Lady Margaret was not of a temperament to be easily deceived, or likely to be dazzled by the specious bait of so illustrious an alliance. He became alarmingly ill with a fever,[2] arising from the distress of mind which overpowered him in their progress to the port of embarkation. This, united to his earnest entreaties, and a representation of the persecutions he had long undergone, so wrought on the feelings of the admiral of Brittany, Jean de Quelenac, and the

[1] Cotton MSS. Dom. A. xviii.
[2] Lobineau's Hist. Bret. tome i. p. 751.

noble Peter de Landois, the Duke of Brittany's treasurer, and favourite minister, that being constrained to wait there for a fair wind, the latter connived at the escape of his charge into the abbey church of the town, from which sanctuary no efforts of the English ambassadors could withdraw him. The Baron Shaundé, a nobleman high in favour with Francis, and warmly attached to the unfortunate Henry, co-operated with Peter de Landois in pleading his cause with their royal master, which they did so effectually, that the eyes of the Duke were fully opened to the true cause of his abduction.[1]

Indignant at finding, by farther inquiry, that his credulity had been imposed on by false promises, he again tendered protection to the noble exile, and withdrew him from the sanctuary of St. Maloes, by pledging his word that all exercise of power should henceforth be limited to his being considered a state prisoner in the Castle of Vannes. To avoid a rupture with the English, however, he was compelled to have him strictly guarded, and faithfully to guarantee his safe custody, though it was accompanied by a promise to the illustrious captive, of courteous and respectful treatment.

The pitiable situation of the imprisoned Richmond, and the efforts made to entice him from

[1] Buck's Ric. III. p. 19.

Brittany, were not unmarked or disregarded by
his affectionate parent. Except, however, by means
of few and secret communications, she was unable
to render him the slightest aid : for the long space
of eight years he continued a captive ; and, during that wearisome time, the mortification, dangers, and difficulties, which he endured, were not
the least among the many trials in the life of
Margaret of Lancaster, which combine to render
her memoirs so remarkable in the annals of biography, so replete with stirring interest in an
historical point of view.

Towards the termination of the period just
alluded to, she was called upon to experience
fresh affliction, by the death of Sir Henry Stafford, her second husband,[1] to whom she had
been united for twenty-two years, and whose attachment and respect were evinced by his leaving
her sole executrix to his will ; as well as by the
anxiety expressed in it, to secure to her all lands
and manors, that were promised to him by his
father, the Duke of Buckingham, on his marriage.

Throughout the whole of this instrument, he
alludes to the Lady Margaret in a manner which
bespeaks his fond affection, styling her " his entirely and best-beloved wife, Margaret Countess
of Richmond ;" and, after bequeathing to her the
residue of all his property, he leaves remembrances

[1] Dugdale's Baronage, i. p. 167.

to his son-in-law, the Earl of Richmond, thus testifying also his paternal regard for the offspring of
his much-loved consort.[1] He expired in the year
1481, having directed his body to be buried
within the church of the college of Plessy, in
Essex, which was founded by Thomas, Duke of
Gloucester, the sixth son of Edward the Third.

It would seem, that, at the time of his death, Sir
Henry Stafford and the Lady Margaret must have
been dwelling at Woking, in Surry, as his will is witnessed by Walter Baker, vicar of that parish; and
it would also appear as if they had long sojourned
there, for he bequeathes to the high altar of the same
church " 10s. for tithes and offerings, forgotten or
withholden, and 20s. for works to the same sacred
edifice." It is somewhat remarkable, that little
should be known of a nobleman so highly connected, and united, for many years, to so conspicuous a character as the subject of this memoir.
Except, however, in relation to his marriage and
death, Sir Humphrey Stafford is scarcely named
in history or the public records during his union
with the Countess of Richmond.

Connected with his household, however, was a
person whose after career is so interwoven with
that of the Lady Margaret and her son, that it
would be an error to omit notice of him at this
particular place. Amongst the few bequests in
Sir Henry Stafford's[1] will was one to " Reginald

[1] See Appendix, C.

Bray, his receiver-general," and an old follower of the Buckingham family. After his master's decease, this trusty adherent was continued in the service of his noble mistress, and made steward of her household; from which it may be inferred, that he held as high a place in the confidence of the Lady Margaret as he had done in the estimation of Sir Henry Stafford.

Time, which had produced so little change in the situation of the banished Richmond, had however effected a material alteration in the general state of affairs in his native land. England was, at this time, recovering from the distractions of civil warfare, and, though jealousy and suspicion still lurked " in the court and in the camp," yet the ferocity which had so debased all ranks of society at the close of the Lancastrian dynasty, had gradually mellowed into more kindly feelings, arising from the gay and thoughtless career which made Edward the Fourth a popular monarch, though deficient in many of the noble qualifications that constitute a good prince. The badges of the Red and White Rose were still borne by the old adherents of each faction, but without exciting that spirit of cruelty which characterised both parties; while the youthful representatives of many noble families, allured by the attractions and gallantry of the King and his fascinating court, abandoned the cause for which

their fathers had bled, and enlisted among the supporters of the house of York.

One of the most distinguished seceders of the
latter class was the young Duke of Buckingham,
nephew of the Lady Margaret's deceased husband,
and who was closely allied to herself by birth, as well
as by marriage, his mother being the daughter of
Edmund, Duke of Somerset, the uncle who succeeded to her father's title. This cousin, who bore
the same maiden name as herself,—that of Margaret
Beaufort, had espoused the valiant Sir Humphery,
son and heir of the Earl of Stafford, who fell at
the battle of St. Albans in 1455, a victim to his
zeal for the Lancastrian cause, leaving an infant
heir of five years old, who eventually succeeded to
the title of Duke of Buckingham, bestowed on his
grandfather by Henry the Sixth. In accordance
with the custom of the age, the wardship of the
young Stafford became at the disposal of the
crown ; and Edward the Fourth, on his accession,
conferred it on his sister, the Duchess of Exeter,[1]
that the Earl might be brought up by her, with an
attachment to the line of York. This view was
borne out by the result ; for Buckingham became
as warmly devoted to the political opponents of
the house of Stafford as his father and grandfather
had been to that of the extinct dynasty. Des-
pairing of her son's release from captivity, and

[1] Dugdale's Baron. vi. 167.

restoration to his country, through the agency of
the subdued Lancastrians, when perpetually wit-
nessing the changes in sentiment which had weaned
from their cause even members of her own family,
the Lady Margaret wisely determined to attempt
effecting a re-union with the Earl of Richmond, by
conciliatory measures towards their former ad-
versaries.

With that strong judgment and acute perception which influenced her conduct in all matters of
emergency, she resolved, henceforth, to lay aside
the rapidly fading distinctions of party, and to add
strength to her son's apparently hopeless cause,
by forming alliances with the most popular, or
most powerful individuals of those times. This
path she could the more consistently pursue, by
reason of the prudence which had ever actuated
her, in checking the assumption of right to the
throne, injudiciously advanced in favour of her
son, by the Lancastrians. For she invariably
sought to dissuade them, by the example of her
own submission to the reigning monarch, from
all open display of Richmond's title, which would
have been equally destructive of their own safety,
as she felt it would be untenable with claims so
indisputable as those on which the House of
York had founded their pretensions to the crown.

In accordance with this policy, the Lady
Margaret, at the expiration of her mourning

for the deceased Sir Henry Stafford, accepted
proposals of marriage from Thomas Lord Stanley, steward of the king's household, and lord
of the Isle of Man ;[1] the Stanley immortalized
by Shakespeare, one of the most renowned
nobles of the realm, and one of the greatest
characters of the age. Great, not from high
ancestry or wealth, though he was the inheritor
of both these, but from the rectitude of conduct which ennobled him in the estimation
of all parties, and rendered him the personal
friend as well as the faithful adherent of his
sovereign.

This nobleman was related to the Lady Margaret in no very remote degree of consanguinity,* and he was also closely allied to her
by marriage, having espoused for his first wife,
the Lady Eleanor Neville,† sister to the re-

[1] Collins's Peerage, vol. ii. p. 63.

* The mother of Thomas Lord Stanley, was daughter and
co-heiress of Sir Robert Goushill, and great-grand-daughter of
Henry Plantagenet, Earl of Lancaster and Derby.

† The connection of the Stanleys with the Nevilles, accounts
for the manner in which the former espoused the interests of the
House of York, attached as their family otherwise must have
been, by relationship to the Lancastrian line. The battle of
Blore Heath in 1459, appears to be the first conflict in which
the Stanley family publicly avowed their hostility to Henry VI.
The execution of Lady Stanley's father, the Earl of Salisbury,
at Pomfret in 1460, confirmed them in their opposition to the

nowned Earl of Warwick, and grand-daughter
of Ralph, Earl of Westmoreland, by Joan de
Beaufort, daughter of John of Gaunt, and
Katherine Swynford. It is said that a dispensation was obtained from the see of Rome before
the marriage, and though no evidence of this
fact has been found, the consanguinity of the
parties (Margaret of Richmond being the first
cousin once removed of the Lady Eleanor Neville,) renders it almost certain that this tradition
in the Stanley family is well founded.

Towards the close of the year 1482, Lord
Stanley espoused the Lady Margaret, and the
official situation of that nobleman as one of the
king's council, obliged her to leave the retirement she had adorned with such dignity, and
which had so long hidden her estimable qualities
from general observation. This change of life,
if not altogether in unison with her austere and
studious habits, yet was one which she unhesitatingly adopted as the only probable method
of effecting her son's release after twelve years'
imprisonment.

Quitting her paternal domains, the vassals appertaining to which she had gladdened by her

Lancastrian cause, and the subsequent marriage of the heir of
the house of Stanley, George Lord Strange, with the sister of
Edward the Fourth's queen, cemented their union with the
reigning family, and fully explains the cause of the zeal with
which they devoted themselves to that monarch and his offspring.

benevolence, and benefited by her charity, the
Lady Margaret removed to Derby House, her
husband's princely abode in London, which he
had recently erected on St. Benet's Hill, where
the Herald's College now stands.[1]   Scarcely, however, was she settled in her new habitation, when
her lord was sent into Scotland with a large force
to aid the Duke of Gloucester at the siege of
Berwick, whence, however, he, together with that
prince, was speedily summoned by the unexpected
demise of Edward the Fourth, in the forty-second
year of his age, and the twenty-second of his reign.
This event effected a greater change in the public
life of the Countess of Richmond, than her marriage with an acknowledged Yorkist had produced
in her domestic career.   Faithful to the late king,
whose confidence and affection he had especially
enjoyed, from having resisted in former times even
the entreaties of his brother-in-law, the renowned
Earl of Warwick,[2] to join the revolt which had
driven Edward from the throne, the Lord Stanley
hastened to the widowed queen, to tender allegiance to her son, and to redeem the pledge he had
given to the deceased monarch, soon after Prince
Edward's birth, that he would maintain his claims
as King of England, in the event of his surviving
his father.   By the death of Edward the Fourth,
his youthful heir became the lawful successor to

---

[1] Pennant's London.   [2] Paston Letters, 2. p. 37.

the throne, and was proclaimed in the month of April by the title of Edward the Fifth, his uncle, the Duke of Gloucester, being nominated Protector of the realm during his minority. [1]

The extraordinary incidents that mark this important year, and which have rendered it one of the most memorable in the annals of our country, are too conflicting, and too important, both in themselves and in their results, to admit even of a brief recapitulation, though the ultimate position of the illustrious subject of this memoir was intimately connected with that wonderful revolution, which, in the brief space of ten weeks, comprehended the proclamation of Edward the Fifth, and the usurpation of Richard the Third, without a single effort to preserve the rights of the true heir, or to check the ambition of the Protector. The chief agent in promoting the election of the latter prince, was Henry Duke of Buckingham, [2] and one of the most powerful of his enemies, and the most faithful adherent of Edward the Fifth, was Thomas Lord Stanley. His fidelity indeed had nearly cost him his life, before the youthful king was deposed, and though preserved from the peril which menaced his person, it was followed by the loss of liberty. The uncompromising and loyal Stanley was committed by the Duke of Gloucester to the Tower, and the actions of his family were

[1] Croyland Chron. 556.   [2] More's Rich. III. p. 253.

jealously watched; but on the election of the Protector to the throne, he was released, and every pains taken to win him to his interests. These proceedings had worked a very powerful change in the domestic sentiments of Lord Stanley and the Countess of Richmond. At the time of their marriage, notwithstanding the strict neutrality observed by the latter in all matters of state, yet their views, it was well known both to themselves and others, were in direct collision ; the negative allegiance of Margaret of Lancaster being strongly contrasted with the positive loyalty of the king's personal friend and servant. The words of Edward the Fourth's queen, as given by Shakspeare are a just epitome of the feeling of the Court towards this illustrious pair at the time of their marriage.

> *Stan.*—God make your majesty joyful as you have been !
> *Q. Elizabeth.*—The Countess Richmond, good my Lord of
>   Stanley,
> To your good prayer will scarcely say—amen.
> Yet, Stanley, notwithstanding she's your wife,
> And loves not me, be you, good lord, assured,
> I hate not you for her proud arrogance.
>   *Stan.*—I do beseech you, either not believe
> The envious slanders of her false accusers ;
> Or, if she be accus'd on true report,
> Bear with her weakness, which, I think, proceeds
> From wayward sickness, and no grounded malice.[1]

[1] Richard III. act i. sc. 3.

I

But a few short months had told deeply on the sympathies of individuals, as well as in the annals of the country. Passive submission to the reigning monarch was now the lot of the noble husband, as for so many years it had been that of his admirable wife; and both were called upon to evince publicly that loyalty which passing events prove to have been so foreign to their private feelings. On the eve of his coronation, the Lord Stanley was created by Richard the Third, Lord Steward of his household;[1] and his personal attendance, as also that of the Lady Margaret his consort, commanded for the ensuing day, to assist at the solemn ceremonial which was to confirm his usurpation. [2]

Obedience to the command of kings at this period of absolute monarchy, was merely a choice between life and death, unless indeed absence from the court gave them time for defiance, or refuge in flight. In the present instance, the distinguished pair were in no situation to hesitate, and the Countess of Richmond was drawn from the unobtrusive path of private life in which she had hitherto moved, to take a public and leading position in the courtly proceedings of Richard the Third.[3]

The coronation of this monarch and his queen

---

[1] Grafton's Chron. p. 799. [2] Hall's Chron. p. 375.

[3] Lodge's Memoir, No. 67.

on the 7th July 1483, was solemnized with greater
splendour than that of any preceding sovereign.
He had espoused, some years previously, (about
1473[1]) Anne,* the youngest daughter and co-

[1] Paston Letters, vol. ii. p. 131.

* The opinion has so long been prevalent that the Lady Anne
Neville was the widow of Prince Edward, Henry Sixth's
son, slain at Tewkesbury, that it may not be considered irrelevant, as her marriage with Richard the Third is noticed in
this memoir, to clear the calumniated Queen from so unfounded and unnatural an accusation, as that of having
espoused the murderer of her husband.   The homicide itself
(See note, p. 80,) has been already disproved, and equally untrue is the tradition of the marriage.   The facts are simply
these.   As a matter of policy, the usual cause of betrothments
in the middle ages, the son of Margaret of Anjou was contracted
in 1470 to the co-heiress of the powerful Warwick, as a bond
of union between two parties, which had previously been so
violently opposed to each other.   The affianced couple were
strangers, and very young, the Prince of Wales but sixteen years
of age; and the sole condition on which the haughty Queen of
Henry VI. was induced to consent to their future marriage
was the recovery, by the Earl of Warwick, of her husband's
crown.   But the compact was never fulfilled, the Lady Anne's
heroic father having fallen at the battle of Barnet, and Prince
Edward being slain shortly afterwards at Tewkesbury.   As a
pledge of his honourable intentions, the Earl of Warwick, on
quitting France, had left his daughter with Margaret of Anjou,
but there is no document which narrates the meeting of the
youthful betrothed, none which attests their marriage.   Neither
does there appear even the probability of such an event having
occurred, for the outlawed Queen was not of a disposition to
sanction, prematurely, an alliance, against which she had pro-
tested as disparaging to the Prince of Wales, and to which she
at last only yielded a reluctant and conditional assent, on ac-

heiress of the famed Earl of Warwick, and who consequently was niece by marriage to the Lord Stanley. This latter nobleman was appointed to bear the staff of Constable before the King, who was attired in robes of purple velvet, having his train borne by the Duke of Buckingham, who also held in his hand the white staff of Lord High Steward of England, an office bestowed on him for life, by Richard the Third, but which he claimed by inheritance from the house of Bohun.*

The Queen followed, apparelled in robes of velvet, with a circlet of gold and precious stones on her head. The honor of supporting Her Majesty's train being allotted to the noble " Margaret of Somerset, Countess of Richmond !"[1] At the banquet which followed in Westminster Hall, the Lord Stanley as Steward, (with three other noblemen belonging to the royal household,) served the

count of her child's hopeless prospects, and at the earnest solicitations of the French Monarch, at whose court she had sought and received an asylum.—(Harl. MSS. 543).

* His great-grandfather, Edmund, had married Ann the daughter of the Duke of Gloucester ; her mother was one of the co-heiresses of Humphrey Bohun, Earl of Hereford. Richard the Third's aversion to grant him the Hereford lands, was from its apparently sanctioning a claim of affinity to Henry the Fourth, and through that to the crown ; Henry the Fifth's mother being the sister of Buckingham's maternal ancestor. — Sharon Turner, vol. iii. p. 502. ·

[1] Baker's Chron. p. 226.

king " with one dish of gold, and another of
silver." A place of marked distinction was allotted to the Lady Margaret, who was ranked
with the princesses of the blood royal, and occupied a station not far removed from the Queen's
person. Her Majesty was served by her honourable
ladies, no gentlemen being with them, except the
carvers, who knelt at their feet ; the peers
being seated apart with the king.[1]   Still further
to ingratiate himself with the head of a family,
whose power he dreaded, and whose allegiance
he coveted, Richard created the Lord Stanley,
towards the close of the same year, Constable of
England for life, investing him with the order of
the Garter, and bestowing on him other marks of
his favour and esteem.[2]

The fair opening which these accumulated
honours gave his illustrious consort to plead the
cause of her banished son, was too favourable to
be overlooked by so devoted and anxious a parent.
She continually supplicated the King to restore
the attainted Earl to his patrimony ; and seizing
on the conciliatory proposition formerly made
(though with subtlety by Edward the Fourth,)
she further urged permission for his union with
one of the deceased monarch's daughters. But
the liberation of the captive Tudor formed no
part of King Richard's policy. In consequence

[1] Leland's Collect. vol. iv. p. 162.   [2] Harl. MSS. 433.

of his usurpation of the throne from the youthful
heir, and the hitherto unexplained disappearance
of both his nephews, the partisans of the house
of York became discontented, so that a scion
of the line of Lancaster, so much feared in less
ominous times, was doubly formidable to a
monarch who knew himself to be unpopular with
both factions.   Immediately after his usurpation,
he despatched Sir Thomas Hutton to renew the
existing treaty with the Duke of Brittany,[1] and
ensure the continued imprisonment of the persecuted Richmond, by sumptuous gifts to his ministers, as well as to himself.   The report of his
ambassador was so satisfactory, that he was
relieved from all fear in that quarter; and he completed his assumption of the sovereignty by creating
Edward, — the young Earl of Salisbury, his only
child, — Prince of Wales, and Duke of Cornwall.[2]

Having thus provided for the safe custody of
his apprehended rival abroad, and secured the
allegiance of his subjects at home, by his recent
coronation, he proceeded in great state to the
ancient city of York, with his queen, his son, and
the chief of his courtiers; where he was a second
time crowned with extraordinary pomp, a circumstance unparalleled since the time of the Anglo

[1] Harl. MSS. 433. p. 241.   [2] Polidore Virgil, 547.

Saxon kings, and constituting one of the most marked features of this king's extraordinary reign.

The ceremony was performed by Dr. Rotheram, Archbishop of that See, with great solemnity. On its termination, Prince Edward, who was about ten years of age, and was led by the hand of the Queen, during the procession through the city, having on his head the coronet of a prince, was created Earl of Chester, and a second time invested with the principality of Wales.[1]

Dispirited at the failure of her efforts after twelve years submissive endurance, and indignant at the implacable rancour, the unceasing persecution, which, without a shadow of blame, had consigned to hopeless imprisonment her unoffending son, the Lady Margaret was roused, at length, to listen to propositions for his emancipation by secret aid, and to countenance measures for obtaining, by force of arms, that justice which had so long, and so ungenerously been denied her.

Shortly after King Richard's coronation at Westminster Abbey, a marked coolness and jealousy arose between him and his coadjutor in the usurpation of the throne, Henry, the powerful Duke of Buckingham. Various motives have been assigned for the bitter feelings which succeeded to the enthusiastic devotion that had

[1] King's Vale Royal, p. 33.

led the Duke to side so strongly with the Protector. The grave details of the chroniclers of
these troubled times, assign[1] more cause for his
change of feelings, than the father of the English
drama, who has handed his name down with such
discredit to posterity, as the selfish betrayer of that
monarch, to whom his vows had recently been
tendered.[2] Buckingham was weak and vain, but
he was the near kinsman, and personal friend of
Richard. Ambition was the rock on which he
struck ; but ingratitude, and breach of faith were
the causes that roused that spirit of indignation
in the impetuous prince which led to open rebellion, and ended in his own utter destruction.

In yielding to the representations of Gloucester,
as regards his usurpation of the throne, it no-
where appears that the noble Duke was actuated
by any hostile feelings towards the young Princes
in the Tower. Their suspicious disappearance,
and the faithless observance of those promises on
which he had relied with full confidence, opened
Buckingham's eyes to the fact of what a mere
tool he had been made, and henceforth converted
Richard's most devoted friend into his bitterest
foe.[3] The true state and origin of the quarrel,
however, are irrelevant to this memoir, though the

[1] Hall's Chron. 387. Grafton, 813. More, 254.
[2] Shakspeare's Rich. III. act iv. scene 2.
[3] Grafton's Chron. 815.

result of their dissension brought over to the
Lancastrian party, an ally as powerful as heretofore he had been deemed successful in the cause
of Richard the Third. Dr. Morton, Bishop of
Ely, who could not be induced to sanction the
disinheritance of the deceased monarch's children,
had early been committed to the custody of his
then political opponent, the Duke of Buckingham, and had continued from the period of his release from the Tower, after the proclamation of King
Richard, a closely watched prisoner at the Duke's
Castle of Brecknock, in Wales. Thither Buckingham himself retired on the King's departure
for York, and there his discontent was speedily
apparent to the irritated and loyal bishop, and
was as speedily fomented into designs of secret
rebellion, and open defiance.[1]

A compact was forthwith effected between
them, the result of which was, that the Duke
should forthwith seek his kinswoman, the Countess of Richmond, propose to her the emancipation of her son from captivity, and enter into
a treaty for seating him on the throne of England,
provided he consented to espouse the Lady Elizabeth of York, who, by the disappearance of the
young Princes, was now the rightful heir. A
singular train of circumstances had rendered this
proposition no less acceptable to the Lord

[1] Grafton, 816.

Stanley as regarded the princess Elizabeth, than
tempting to the Lady Margaret, by fostering
expectations for the speedy release of her son
from imprisonment, and justifying the hopes
so long fixed on him by the persecuted and
exiled Lancastrians.

On the testimony of a metrical narrative, preserved in the Harleian MSS.[1] the production
of Humphrey Brereton, a gentleman apparently
of some talent and acquirement, and who held a
trustworthy situation in the service of Lord
Stanley, it appears that King Edward, on his
death bed, confided to the especial care of this
eminent nobleman his eldest daughter Elizabeth.

This young Princess had early been affianced
to the Dauphin of France, whose offensive breach
of the contract by his recent marriage with the
grand-daughter of the Emperor of Germany,
had incensed to the highest degree the late
king, who was preparing to avenge the affront by
war with that country, when his sudden and fatal
illness terminated his career.

The Lady Elizabeth, thus prematurely bereft
of her royal father, is stated to have lodged in
Derby House under the protection of the Lord
Stanley,[2] after quitting the sanctuary in West-

[1] Harleian MSS. 367.
[2] See Privy Purse expences of Elizabeth of York, by
Sir Harris Nicolas, p. 56.

minster Abbey, in which her distressed mother
had taken refuge with her children on the arrest
of her brother, Earl Rivers, and the execution of
himself, and other of her kindred at Pomfret ; an
atrocity which made the unhappy Queen first
suspect the ultimate intentions of the Duke of
Gloucester.

The Lord Stanley is especially named as having attended the funeral obsequies of his late
royal master,[1] and his imprisonment so shortly after
the solemn ceremony is of itself sufficient proof
of his fidelity to Edward the Fourth and his offspring. By that monarch he was left one of the
executors of his will :[2] and the care of the Princess Elizabeth, whose extreme beauty was heightened by the gentleness and winning sweetness of
her temper,[3] is said to have completed the devotion
which though cherished in secret, bound him
unalterably to the deceased king's children. After
his release, the suspicious watchfulness of King
Richard precluded any open espousal of their
cause, which indeed was beset with difficulty of
all kinds, and rendered little short of hopeless by
the doubtful fate of Edward the Fifth, and the
youthful Richard, his brother.

On the departure of the King and Queen for
York, it is probable that the Countess of Rich-

[1] Harl. MSS. 6. 111.   [2] Royal Wills, p. 347.
[3] Bernard Andreas MS.

mond quitted the metropolis to visit her estates in the Midland counties, for it is recorded that whilst journeying between Worcester and Bridgnorth,[1] she was met by the Duke of Buckingham on his mission.

He then communicated to her the important league which had been formed between himself and Bishop Morton, through which the reported death of the young Princes was to be avenged, and peace restored to the country, by the union of the two eldest surviving branches of the Plantagenet family. The Lady Margaret promised her zealous co-operation towards effecting an object so desirable for the realm, and so grateful to her maternal pride. In her eyes King Richard was a usurper, and a regicide; and her son and the Lady Elizabeth martyrs to an unjust ambition: hence, the yearning affection which led her so ardently to desire the deliverance of her child, warred not with any religious compunctions towards the reigning monarch. That she would have withheld her consent, had it been otherwise, is probable, from the meekness and forbearance with which she submitted to the oppressive treatment of the Earl of Richmond by his predecessor, Edward the Fourth, who, however opposed to her politically or individually, she nevertheless considered her lawful sovereign.

[1] Baker's Chron. p. 229.

While the Duke of Buckingham proceeded on his journey to open the plot to other adherents of the deceased king, the Lady Margaret undertook to communicate it to the Queen Dowager, through the medium of her physician, Dr. Lewis,[1] a Welshman devoted to her interests, and those of her son, and who from his profession had ready access to every branch of the royal family.

During Buckingham's absence from Brecknock Castle, on this grave mission, the bishop's escape (at which he connived) was effected. Proceeding direct to Ely, by the most unfrequented route, he abstracted a considerable sum of money secreted in his abode there, and journeying hence with all speed to the sea-side, the prelate effected a safe landing in France, from whence he passed in disguise into Brittany, and announced to the Earl of Richmond the bright prospects that had at length dawned on him. Richard the Third, was a man of too deep discernment to be entirely blinded, notwithstanding the guarded conduct and cautious measures observed by his enemies. He had narrowly watched their actions, and had certain intelligence of their proceedings. He knew what friends and supporters had pledged themselves to his rival, though many of them maintained a semblance of allegiance to himself. Nevertheless it suited his purpose to conceal his

[1] Polydore Virgil, p. 549.

knowledge, until the whole plot was more fully developed. The Queen Dowager entered with alacrity into the scheme communicated by Dr. Lewis, promising on her part to engage the co-operation of the most influential of the Yorkist party, if Henry of Richmond by solemn oath would bind himself to marry her daughter Elizabeth, whose consent to the compact she readily obtained, and whose pledge was forthwith forwarded to him.[1] While matters were thus progressing in England, the banished Earl was zealously advancing his interests in foreign courts. He first pleaded his cause frankly with the Duke of Brittany; but his league with King Richard which in honour he could not violate, precluded Francis from openly affording him aid. He was nevertheless so affected by his tale, and won over by his entreaties, that he promised to offer no opposition to his undertaking, if he would raise sufficient force to attempt the restitution of his alleged rights.

With other potentates, Richmond was still more successful; they promised him active assistance, and so zealously espoused his cause, and encouraged him with such flattering assurances of support, that by the close of the eventful year that witnessed Richard's usurpation of the crown, Henry Tudor had drawn to his party so many

[1] Harl. MSS. 367.

powerful princes, and was supported by so strong
a band both of Yorkists, and Lancastrians, that
the spring of 1484 dawned with hopes that bid
fair to reward both himself and his mother for
their many years of painful separation. But —
prosperity and peace were yet far distant.

In the January of that year, Richard the Third
assembled parliament, in which, after noticing the
Earl of Richmond's pretensions to the crown,
and his attempts to engage the King of France
and Duke of Brittany on his behalf, he caused
him to be attainted of high treason,[1] together
with Jasper Tudor, Earl of Pembroke, Morton, Bishop of Ely, and all the other partizans
of the illustrious captive. The Lady Margaret
was declared to have merited a sentence equally
severe for " sending writings, tokens, money, and
messages to the Earl, her son, stirring him up to
invade the realm ;" but fear of the powerful
family with whom she was now allied obtained for
the Countess of Richmond, a lenity which Margaret of Lancaster if unprotected, would vainly have
sought from Richard the Third. In consideration
of the services which the Lord Stanley had rendered to the House of York, the king forbore to
attaint the Countess; but she was banished the
Court, and ordered to be closely confined to her
husband's residence in the country ; and an act of

[1] Rot. Parl. vol. vi. p. 246.

parliament declared her lands to be forfeited, degraded her from all titles of dignity, and settled her property on her consort for his life, with remainder to the crown at his decease.[1]

This public denouncement of a combination formed secretly, and pursued with extreme caution, paralysed for a brief period the exertions of all connected with the scheme. The Lord Stanley had throughout maintained a strict neutrality. He wisely concealed his real sentiments at this critical juncture, though his zeal for the cause of the late king's offspring appears never to have been diminished either by bribes, as relates to personal aggrandisement, or threats, which were made more significant by the public disgrace, and the forfeiture of the title and lands of his illustrious consort. He was the first to disclose his fears of the Duke of Gloucester's evil designs on the youthful Princes;[2] but Lord Stanley's knowledge of human nature, and experience in the vacillation of public opinion in those troubled times, taught him that tranquil submission would better serve the deceased monarch's family than indiscreet zeal, or premature assertion of rights.

Amongst the number of eminent persons, whom we have noticed as commiserating the situation of Henry Tudor, was Margaret, Duchess of Brittany.

---

[1] Rot. Parl. vi. p. 244.   [2] More's Rich. III. p. 199.

Of her he now earnestly besought assistance. Though deaf to the expostulations and fervent prayer of his prisoner, Francis could not withstand the urgent solicitations of his consort. She succeeded in obtaining both liberty and aid for the captive Richmond, and three ships well furnished with men, arms, and provisions were placed at his disposal.

The valiant Buckingham, whose power and influence was very great, had raised so strong a force in Wales, that being joined by the kindred of the dowager queen, the Earl of Devon, and some of the most distinguished persons of the age, he openly unfurled the standard of rebellion, and vowed defiance to the king. But the elements seemed again to conspire against the ill-fated Richmond, and fortune to befriend the usurper. Having assembled, by the aid of foreign allies, forty ships, with five hundred paid mercenaries, he sailed from Brittany on the 4th October 1484, making for Poole, in Dorset, before which port he anchored, that by means of spies, he might discover the position of King Richard's army, and of his own allies. Finding that part of the coast strongly guarded, he again put to sea, to proceed westward. Scarcely, however, had he lost sight of land, than so awful a tempest arose, that on the same night his little fleet was totally dispersed, and all his bright hopes

K

again laid low.   In the fearful darkness that prevailed, great part of the vessels foundered and were wholly lost; the remnants were scattered, some on the shores of Brittany, others on those of France.

The Earl of Richmond himself narrowly escaped with life, and was cast on the coast of Normandy, whence sending messengers to Charles the Eighth, King of France, he was kindly invited to his court, and aided with sums of money towards defraying the charge of his ill-fated expedition.   Returning after a time into Brittany, to renew with a heavy heart his amicable understanding with Duke Francis, he there found fresh affliction awaiting him.   His expectations in England being annihilated by the execution of the Duke of Buckingham, and the total dispersion of his army by long continued storms, and unexampled floods.   The calamity which had visited the Earl of Richmond on the sea, had fallen with equal ruin on his English allies : for so unceasing had been the rain, so fearful the tempest, that the Severn which the Duke of Buckingham had to cross, to reach the coast for the reception of Richmond, became impassable.

It overflowed the adjoining lands, to an amazing extent, and, for ten days, the country on each side was so deluged, that his troops were exposed to the severest privations of hunger and wretchedness. Alarmed at such a fearful visitation, the Welch soldiery, considering it an ill omen,[1] abandoned their noble leader, and, in spite of his earnest entreaties, dispersed to a man, and quietly returned to their homes.

The princely Buckingham himself was compelled to seek shelter at a farm house near Shrewsbury,[2] with a servant, whom he had fostered, for years, with extreme kindness; but, alas! the perfidy he had shewn to Edward the Fifth, and which he was about to repeat, though with some shew of reason, towards Richard the Third, was repaid with signal vengeance on his own head. The large sum speedily offered by the King for his apprehension,[3] was a golden bait not to be resisted by his treacherous and mercenary follower. " The deep revolving witty Buckingham" was disgracefully betrayed by the worthless Banaster to the High Sheriff of Shropshire, who conveyed him to Salisbury, where the King was then encamped. A scaffold was immediately erected in the market place of that city, and, without trial, the noble Duke was there beheaded on the 2nd of November, 1483, having first earnestly, but fruitlessly, besought an interview with King Richard. These complicated miseries greatly dispirited Henry of Richmond; but being gradually joined

[1] Baker's Chron. p. 236.
[2] Polydore Virgil, p. 552.   [3] Rymer's Fed. xii. 204.

by such of the leaders of Buckingham's army as had escaped the storms, their enthusiasm in his cause inspired him with fresh energy; and, having rallied from the disheartening effects of their discomfiture, they proceeded on Christmas day, in solemn state to the cathedral at Rheims, and, before the high altar, the Earl renewed his oath to espouse the Princess Elizabeth, all the assembled warriors pledging themselves, most sacredly, never to cease prosecuting war against King Richard until either his deposition or destruction was effected.

The English Monarch had not slumbered during this period. In the Parliament which he assembled on the 23rd of January, 1484, he caused the crown to be settled upon him, and the heirs of his body,[1] the children of his elder brother, the Duke of Clarence being declared incapable of succession, by reason of their father's attainder; and the family of Edward the Fourth, having already been excluded, on the ground of illegitimacy, arising from the pretended informality of his marriage,[*] that king having been pre-contracted to Lady Eleanor Butler,[2] when the beautiful

[1] Act of Settlement. Rot. Parl. vi. 241.   [2] More, 241.

[*] By the ancient canon law, a contract for marriage might be valid and perfect without the church ceremony; and second marriages were liable to be annulled on account of the existence of a pre-contract, until the statute of 32 Hen. VIII. rescinded the same.—Sharon Turner, iii. p. 463.

widow of Lord Grey tempted the gallant monarch to forego his engagements, and privately to make her his queen.

In a proclamation, issued a few months after this extraordinary proceeding of King Richard's, the widow of the deceased monarch is styled " Dame Elizabeth Grey, late calling herself Queen of England."[1] Still more firmly to establish his own claims, and to perpetuate them in his family, he caused the principal personages of his kingdom to swear adherence and fidelity to his son Edward, the young Prince of Wales.[2] He likewise vigilantly guarded the sea-coast, to prevent the sudden landing of the Earl of Richmond, and dispersed spies throughout the country to gather information relative to persons favouring the Lancastrian cause. He had divers individuals executed, and he attainted all such as were in exile with Richmond, seizing their lands and goods, and appropriating them to his own use.

To defeat yet more effectually the views of his opponents as regarded the union of the two Roses, he determined himself to espouse the Lady Elizabeth of York, the decline of the Queen, apparently in consumption, giving speedy prospect of his widowhood. The match he proposed was one unexampled in the history of this country, on account of the near consanguinity of the parties as uncle and

[1] Harl. MSS. p. 308.   [2] Chron. Croy. p. 570.

niece; but it was King Richard's object to darken the prospects of Richmond, by casting into the shade his brightest hopes, and defeating, by vigilance, those plans which were daily forming in favour of his rival.

The consequence of this most unnatural design was to effect a marked relaxation in the severe treatment hitherto exercised towards the family of Edward the Fourth.[1]   The appearance of the Lady Elizabeth at court was immediately required, where she was forthwith placed in attendance on the Queen; and the young princesses, her sisters, were soon after withdrawn from the sanctuary at the Abbey, by promises of the King's favour and advancement, and were received during festivities at Westminster Hall with marked courtesy and honourable distinction, both by Richard the Third and his royal consort.

A grievous blow, however, was in store for the King; one which was to wound him in the tenderest point, and to lay prostrate those schemes of future ambition for which he had sacrificed so much of honour and humanity. He had calculated on the death of his wife, whom the physicians had pronounced to be past recovery, but he had not anticipated that the melancholy event would have been preceded by the demise of his only child, the young Prince of Wales, who expired at Middle-

[1] Buck's Rich. III. p. 127.

ham Castle the 9th of April, 1484, in the twelfth
year of his age.[1] The languor and debility of Queen
Anne was increased by this unlooked-for affliction ; she survived her son but a few months, and
died, not of poison, as has been asserted, and so
long unjustly credited,—as if King Richard had
perpetrated every crime that malignity could lay
to his charge,—but from the effects of a lingering
decline, accelerated by grief at the premature
death of her child. Thus was Richard the Third
left childless and a widower, apparently, in the
plenitude of his success, and thus were the views
of his opponents more strongly advanced by the
retributive justice of Heaven. These most unlooked-for events rekindled anew those embers
of dissatisfaction and rebellion, which had only
smouldered, but never been extinguished in the
minds of either faction. The treaty of marriage,
said to have been proposed between King
Richard and his niece, the Princess Elizabeth,
before the demise of the Queen, had completely
alienated from him the affections of the Yorkist
party : while the nomination of John, the young
Earl of Lincoln, son of his eldest sister, Elizabeth, as heir apparent to the throne, roused a
spirit of indignation in the baffled Lancastrians,
too strong ever again to be put down.

It may not be uninteresting here to remark,

[1] Chron. Croyland, p. 571.

that the noble individual thus elevated, by the decease of the Prince of Wales, to so exalted a position, was the lineal descendant of Philippa Py-
card, wife of the poet Geoffrey Chaucer,[1] who has
been already noticed as the sister to Katherine
Swynford ; and as *domicella* to the Queen of Edward the Third, at the period when her sister filled
the same situation about the person of the Lady
Blanch, of Lancaster.[2] Thus, by one of those
extraordinary revolutions which renders historical
research so interesting, by proving that the romance of real life is as replete with incident as the
most highly wrought production of mere human
ingenuity — the lineal descendants of the two
sisters were at this epoch brought into collision,
as heirs of the long contested throne.

Remarkable, indeed, was the situation of the
progeny of the co-heiresses of Sir Payne de
Roet, at this eventful period of English history.
The young Earl of Lincoln, whom King Richard,
in default of male issue, had procured to be nominated as his successor to the crown, in right of his
mother, the Lady Elizabeth Plantagenet, sister to
himself, and the late King Edward, was the fourth
in direct descent from Philippa, the wife of Geoffrey
Chaucer ; whilst the Earl of Richmond stood in
exactly the same degree of relationship to Katherine Swynford, her sister, who, by the ultimate

[1] Hollinshed, A.D. 1484.   [2] Godwin, vol. iv, p. 161.

succession of King Henry the Seventh, became the
ancestress of all the future sovereigns of England.

To return, however, from this brief digression.
—King Richard renewed his proposals of marriage to his niece in due form immediately after
the late Queen's interment ;[1] and to the astonishment of all men, notwithstanding the barrier of
their near relationship, he overcame the Queen
Dowager's scruples, who, unmindful of her oath
to the Countess of Richmond, and regardless of
the King's treatment of her family, consented
for an application to the Pope to sanction the
union.[2] The pitiable situation in which this unhappy princess was placed, bereft of her sons,
and mourning the execution of her nearest
kindred, scarcely rendered her a free agent ; and
terror lest the committal of her daughters to the
Tower, might be the result of refusal, justifies the
conclusion both reasonably and in charity, that
her alleged consent was extorted by maternal
fear, and her scruples laid at rest by the confident
hope, that neither the See of Rome, nor the
English nation would submit to so unnatural
and revolting a marriage. The love of life
inherent in the youthful breast, united to that
firm trust in her God, which had marked the
character[3] of this amiable princess from her cradle,

[1] Dr. Lingard's Hist. Eng. vol. v. p. 355.
[2] Baker's Chron. p. 231.   [3] Ber. And. in Cotton : MS.

may as satisfactorily account for the letter, said
to be extant in the archives of the Norfolk family,[1]
from the Lady Elizabeth of York, in which she
professes attachment to King Richard, and
anxiety to promote their union, though her vows
had been secretly made to his rival, and her
pledge[2] forwarded in token of her fidelity. Alas!
for England's honor, at this most degraded period
of her national history. Deceit, intrigue, and
treachery like a blight, had blackened the whole
face of nature, and rendered undistinguishable
by means of its withering effects, the wholesome
fruits of the land, from such as were irrecoverably
diseased and worthless. There are strong reasons
to believe from manuscripts of that period,[3] that
King Richard had no actual intent to celebrate
so extraordinary a marriage, but that his aim in
propounding it was to divert the affections of his
niece, and to nullify that policy which involved
his own destruction, by the proposed union of
the two Roses, in the persons of their rightful
representatives, the Lady Elizabeth of York,
and the exiled Henry of Lancaster. All parties,
however, were too highly excited to render any
cessation of hostility practicable, by mere acts of
policy. Ten months of bitter exasperation followed the death of Buckingham, and the defeat

---

[1] Buck's Rich. III. p. 129.   [2] Harl. MSS. 367.
[3] Chron. Croy. 572.

of Richmond's proposed invasion ; it was passed by the remnant of the Plantagenets on both sides, in gathering a sufficient force to decide by the sword the long protracted quarrel, each faction being resolved to extinguish the other.

During this eventful period, the Lady Margaret was not an inactive spectator. No longer Countess of Richmond, in consequence of the act which deprived her of title and lands, she felt herself absolved from all allegiance to the king, and at liberty to follow the dictates of maternal interests. Through the medium of Christopher Urswicke, her chaplain and confessor, Hugh Conway, a zealous Lancastrian, and Reginald Bray, the trusty follower before alluded to, she privately supplied her son with large sums of money, and despatched emissaries to rouse the co-operation of the friends and connections of their persecuted house. In consequence of these proceedings, the Lord Stanley,[1] though abstaining from all apparent interference, began to be suspected by Richard the Third, as a well-wisher to the interest of his consort and her son. He was commanded to dismiss all her old servants, and forbidden to communicate with, or receive messages from the Earl of Richmond. The situation of this powerful nobleman was singularly distressing, for on his discretion seemed to hang the lives of his wife,

[1] Seacombe's House of Stanley.

and possibly of the young princess, the preservation of both of whom were so material towards
the fulfilment of a scheme he had almost as much
at heart as the Lady Margaret; deeming with
her, that by the union of the objects of their
mutual love, peace would at length be restored to
the distracted kingdom. He was constrained
therefore to act a part, and to remain perfectly
passive, though it appears by the statement of
Humphrey Brereton, his esquire, that he had
constant communication with the young princess
on the subject, whose pathetic remonstrances, it
is the burden of his narrative to prove, was
the true cause of the Lord Stanley's taking
eventually so decided a part against King Richard;
despite of the peculiar circumstances which to
the last moment, compelled him to appear a
partizan of his cause. The trusty Brereton was
sent into Cheshire to communicate with Lord
Stanley's sons, and to state the noble chieftain's
sentiments to his valiant brother, Sir William
Stanley of Holt, and other of their connections,
urging them to be prepared for active measures,
in case of the Earl of Richmond's landing in
Wales. Passing by a circuitous route into
Brittany, he was the bearer of letters both from
the young princess and Lord Stanley to the
exiled Tudor, together with a ring from the
former in testimony of her continued fidelity.

This faithful follower, who states himself to have been privy to the motives, as well as agent to the designs of his noble employer, has thrown much interesting light on the proceedings of this confused era. Many of his statements in verse are corroborated by the prose annals of Grafton, the earliest typographical collector of English annals, and who treated especially of the union of the houses of York and Lancaster. All countries are more or less indebted for the preservation of their early historical events to the rude poetical effusions of primitive times. From the Armorican and ancient British rhymes, Geoffrey of Monmouth, compiled his chronicle of the native princes of our island, which account, if obscured by much fable, and garnished with romantic legend, contains nevertheless facts sufficiently well attested to be quoted as authority by Hume, and other standard historians. The rude verses of early monkish writers, supplied materials to Spenser, Shakspeare, and other of our best poets for their sublime compositions. Lydgate's poetical works were chiefly on historical subjects; and the immortal Milton, after publishing in prose, a history of England to the Norman invasion, became so fascinated with his metrical authorities that he formed the design of perpetuating in an epic poem, the rhyming traditions of that early period.[1]

[1] Johnson's Lives of the Poets.

The character of Bishop Morton and other prominent actors of the troubled times of which this narrative treats, have been faithfully and minutely traced in Dr. John Hird's Metrical History of England,[1] and posterity is so entirely indebted for the preservation of various important national occurrences to lyrical compositions, from the time of the wandering minstrel until the age of chivalry had passed away, that the statements of Humphrey Brereton being written in poetic measure, does not invalidate his testimony; while many of his assertions are unquestionable and impart authority to the whole. Greater stress has been laid on the confidence to be attached to the statements of Humphrey Brereton, from the elucidation which his narrative affords to apparent acts of intrigue and double dealing, peculiarly irreconcileable as emanating from individuals so eminent for piety, rectitude, and high principles, as Lord Stanley and the Lady Margaret. They have been accused of acting a treacherous and ensnaring part to the monarch they ostensibly professed to serve, whereas it would appear, that fidelity to the trust reposed in him by his deceased sovereign, and unchangeable devotion for his offspring, influenced every action of Lord Stanley from his imprisonment before the deposition of the young king, to his efforts for the restoration

[1] Buck's Rich. III. p. 52.

of his rights in the person of his eldest sister;
while to a mind constituted like that of the
Countess of Richmond, the vices imputed to
Richard the Third, must have excited such horror
and detestation, that she needed not the plea of
maternal affection, or the instigation of her priestly
confessor Urswicke, to believe that in endeavouring to effect the restitution of the Lancastrian
line she was promoting the ends of justice; and
accelerating the retribution of Heaven on the
head of an acknowledged usurper — a suspected
regicide and murderer. And here Brereton's
narrative also helps to explain the apparently
inconsistent conduct of King Richard, who
wooing his niece before his wife's death, did not
marry her when that obstacle was removed. The
princess herself, whose proximity to the throne
rendered her the tool of both factions, is cleared
by the same authority from desiring a union,
which, if true, would deteriorate from the singular virtues which all parties unite in ascribing to
her ; by showing that though the fear of being
doomed to her brother's untimely end, induced a
seeming compliance with the will of her mother,
yet that it was in truth a feeling wholly sub-
servient to that confident belief and trust in
her Heavenly Maker, a trait which renders the
character of Elizabeth of York one of the most
endearing that ever graced our regal annals. But,

as before stated, there can be little doubt that
each of the parties were dissembling; the monarch with the purpose of defeating the plans
of Richmond, and his Lancastrian supporters;
the Dowager Queen, and the princess, because
opposition to King Richard's will would have
been as fruitless as they knew it to be dangerous.

On his return from his mission in Brittany, Humphrey Brereton states that he found the Lady
Elizabeth in London, as was likewise Lord Stanley,
to whom he gave so favourable an account of
Richmond's preparations, that his noble father-
in-law felt the period had now arrived for retiring
into the country, that he might be prepared to
co-operate with his illustrious consort in furthering
the views of her son.

But the politic Richard was too well aware of
the powerful resources of the Stanleys, to lose
sight of the head of that wealthy family.　Sus-
pecting that his design was to afford aid to his
rival, an opinion fully proved by the result, he
positively refused his consent to dispense with
his personal attendance, or to his quitting the metropolis even for a brief period, unless he gave up
his son and heir, George Lord Strange, as a hostage for his fidelity : an exaction which placed the
enthralled chieftain in a yet more painful position,
as, by this pledge, another life, if not yet more

precious, was rendered dependent on his circum-
spection for liberty and existence.

Henry of Richmond had found it very difficult
to gain assistance a second time, either from
France or Brittany, in consequence of the utter
failure of his former expedition ; but the romance,
which attached to his singular career, excited so
great an interest in the Lady Anne of Valois,
eldest sister of Charles the Eighth, that female
commiseration once more won for the exiled Earl
that help which his own manly entreaties had
failed of procuring.   In the present instance, few
allies could have befriended him more effectually
than this advocate for his cause. The Lady Anne
was the Princess Royal of France, and so early
distinguished for genius, sagacity, and penetration,
that the reins of government were delegated to her
by Louis the Eleventh, during the minority of his
son, under the title of Governess of France.   The
illustrious Princess, married to the Sire de Beaujeu, youngest brother of the Duke of Bourbon,
and Lieutenant-General of France, was so zealous
in the cause of the persecuted Earl, that she succeeded in obtaining from her brother's ministers
the aid of 3,000 men, and the loan of a considerable sum of money.[1]   But fortune seemed
never weary of overclouding every bright gleam
of sunshine that dawned on the prospects of the
unfortunate Henry Tudor.

[1] Philip de Comines, p. 536.

While the King of France was collecting his promised troops, the Earl returned into Brittany, to communicate the result to his adherents, and to seek further aid from a quarter where he believed a friendly welcome awaited him; but it was far otherwise. His league with France had broken his interest in Brittany. His former friend, Peter de Landois, and the Duke, were so jealous of his residence at the French court, (the Lady of Beaujeu being particularly obnoxious to them,)[1] that they resolved to prevent his proposed invasion of England, by detaining him, as heretofore, a prisoner at Vannes, so soon as preparations were complete for his departure.

Misfortune, however, and continued disappointment in every possible form, had rendered Richmond singularly wary and suspicious. Having received secret intimation of this treachery,[2] he privately charged his uncle, Jasper Tudor, who had been the companion of his exile, and the faithful sharer of his vicissitudes, to march to the confines of Brittany, with the small force already collected, and there to await his coming, and the junction of the French auxiliaries. He remained quietly at Vannes, without shewing his knowledge of the duplicity intended; but, in the course of a few days, under pretence of visiting a friend in an adjoining village, he proceeded, with only five attendants, to

[1] Buck's Rich. III. p. 57.   [2] Dugdale's Baron. ii. p. 239.

a short distance, when suddenly entering a
wood, he assumed the garb of a page, and, continuing his flight with great rapidity during the
night, he reached Anjou, and was joined by his
uncle and troops in France, before the treacherous
Bretons were conscious of his departure from
Vannes. He proceeded forthwith to the French
Court, again to claim the protection of Charles;
and, being courteously received, and finding him
constant to his promises, he took his leave, for a
time; to strengthen his cause by assembling as
leaders to his hired troops, the exiled and dispersed
chieftains, who so long had been banished from
their lands and their home. He commenced by
releasing the Earl of Oxford from the Castle of
Hammes who had there been committed by Edward
the Fourth, but was now set at liberty by Richmond, through the influence of Bishop Morton
with his keeper.

With the exception of these two notices of his
proceedings, the English, Flemish, and French
historians, are altogether silent as to Richmond's
place of abode, after his perilous adventure in
Brittany; but contemporary Welsh bards assert,
that he privately passed from France into Wales,
and there lay concealed, wandering in disguise
from place to place, to ascertain, by personal observation, how the people stood affected towards

[1] Pennant's Wales, vol. i. p. 9.

Richard, and whether he might venture, with prudence, to attempt, as strenuously advised by Reginald Bray, a landing amongst his kindred. Many wild and beautiful compositions are yet extant, in which, under the emblem of the Eagle and the Lion, according to the allegorical poetry of the age, his sojourn is described; and the fact of secret intimation of his proceedings having been communicated to King Richard, is also made known, by a tradition yet preserved in the Mostyn family,—to the effect, that while preparing for dinner with the chief of that house, he was so nearly surprised by the king's soldiery, in their search after him, that an open window alone ensured his escape. To this day, his hiding-place at Tremostyn retains the appellation of the " King's Hole."

Certain it is, that all things were ready for his invasion of England, before he again appeared in France,[1]—when he presented himself suddenly at Paris, to take leave of the King and Madame de Beaujeu: after which, towards the end of July, 1485, he departed for Harfleur, in Normandy, where his shipping lay, and his soldiers were encamped. He there found Bray, awaiting his arrival, with large sums of money from England; and, in addition to his French auxiliaries, 2,000 Bretons, suitably provided, were tendered to his

[1] Buck's Rich. III. p. 58.

acceptance, by Duke Francis,[1] accompanied by
protestations and excuses for his meditated detention; a supply, in all probability, obtained
through his consort, Margaret of Brittany, who
possessed great influence over her husband, and had
so firmly stood his advocate on a former occasion.

Prior to joining his followers, the Earl rested at
Rouen, on his road from Paris to Harfleur, where
he received information, for the first time, that
preparations were making for the immediate union
of King Richard with his affianced bride, the Princess Elizabeth, and also of the actual marriage of
her second sister, the Lady Cicely Plantagenet.
The latter union had been arranged more effectually
to frustrate all hopes of his connection with the co-
heiresses of Edward the Fourth: and, with a view
of increasing his mortification, this young Princess
was bestowed by her uncle, on the Lady Margaret's maternal brother, the son of the Duchess of
Somerset, by her third husband, Leo Lord Welles,[2]
a young man of no pretensions for so high an
alliance, though of ancient and noble family.
Goaded to the quick by the final discomfiture of
his interests in the point where he had chiefly relied for success, and indignant at the vacillation of
the Princess, whose ring he had received in token
of her faith,[3] Richmond, nevertheless, felt that

[1] Dugdale's Baron. tom. ii. p. 240.
[2] Camden's Britt. vol. i, p. 567.   [3] Harleian MSS. 367.

matters had now proceeded too far to admit of any
check of the expected invasion, to which he was
pledged both to his hired troops and to his partizans
in England. As his greatest power lay in Wales,
a country endeared to him as the land of his birth
and childhood, he resolved, in the event of his
contemplated marriage with the Lady Elizabeth
of York not being completed, to strengthen his
connection in that principality, by allying himself to the daughter of his former guardian, Sir
William Herbert ;[1] the companion of his youthful
days, whose brother Sir Walter ranked among the
most powerful of the British chieftains. Dispatch-
ing a trusty messenger with proposals to the latter,
he proceeded, without delay, to Harfleur, carefully concealing from his adherents his chagrin,
and the failure of his views on the House of York,
as also his measures for effecting a fresh alliance
among his early connections.

He sailed from Harfleur on the 7th of August,
and landed shortly after at Milford Haven, in Pembrokeshire, whence he marched by Haverfordwest
to Cardigan, where he was welcomed by his British
kindred with the greatest enthusiasm, the Welsh
hailing him as a Prince descended from the ancient
rulers of the land.   Here the messenger, who had
been dispatched to Sir Walter Herbert, joined him
with the dispiriting intelligence that he found

[1] Grafton's Chron.

it impossible to proceed, for Herbert, having espoused the cause of King Richard, had raised all his power to oppose Richmond.[1]

This unlooked-for intelligence, like many temporary disappointments, proved a blessing, not only to himself, but to the great cause to which Henry of Richmond stood pledged, as it left him free to fulfil those vows which alone ensured him success, by gaining to his party the strength of the Yorkist faction, who had long viewed Richard as an apostate to their cause, and a traitor, by reason of his perfidy to the deceased monarch's sons. Nevertheless, the determined opposition of Sir Walter Herbert, with whom, in boyhood, he had been so intimately associated, made a powerful and very painful impression on the Earl; and so effectually alienated his regard, that on gaining the crown, he deprived him of his lands, and settled them on Cicely, the sister for whose hand he had tendered proposals.[2]   She was eventually married to Sir Charles Somerset; her sister Maud, designed for him in childhood by her father, had previously married Henry, Earl of Northumberland, who proved one of Richmond's most powerful supporters at this trying period.

From Cardigan he sent messengers to the Lady Margaret, his mother, as also to her husband, Lord Stanley, desiring them to meet him on his

[1] Leland's Itin. vol. vi. p. 30.   [2] Dugdale's Baronage.

way, that he might take their advice, as to his future proceedings. The undisguised preparations, so long making by Henry, had roused King Richard to a sense of his danger, and feeling secure of the fidelity of Stanley, from having kept his son as an hostage, he had sent him to Wales as soon as Lord Strange was in his custody, to levy forces, as a farther test of his loyalty.[1]   That nobleman proceeded to Leicester, accompanied, as Brereton states, by the Princess Elizabeth, who, for greater security, was soon after sent, by command of the King, to the castle of Sheriff Hutton, in Yorkshire.   The Lord Stanley and his formidable body of troops, consisting of 5,000 men, all determined and well-disciplined Welsh, continued at Leicester, in which city he was abiding when Reginald Bray privately conveyed to him the Earl of Richmond's message.

Not daring, however, to meet his son-in-law openly, lest his defection might prove the death warrant of Lord Strange, he was constrained, after receiving intimation of his close vicinity, to dissemble his knowledge of the fact, until after night-fall ; when cautiously quitting Leicester, he proceeded to Alderton, about six miles from Redmore Heath, where the hostile armies had encamped.   There under cover of the darkness, in a spot the most lonely that could be selected, the

---

[1] Seacombe's Hist. of Stanley.

interview, rendered so interesting by our great dramatic poet, took place between the son and the husband of Margaret of Lancaster.[1]

> *Richmond.*—" All comfort that the dark night can afford,
>   Be to thy person, noble father-in-law !
>   Tell me how fares our loving mother ?"
> *Stanley.*—" I, by attorney, bless thee from thy mother,
>   Who prays continually for Richmond's good."[2]

This meeting, however, had nearly proved fatal in its consequence to all parties; the Earl of Richmond, from the darkness of the night, mistook the path, and, being unfortunately separated from his attendants, well nigh fell a victim to that ill fortune, which ever seemed at hand to mar his brightest and most cheering prospects. Nevertheless, after great difficulty, he regained his camp in safety, and spent the remainder of the night, which was that of the Sabbath, in earnest and fervent prayer.

The 22nd of August, 1485, was a portentous day for England. To the combatants it was a struggle for life or death—to the leaders a contest for a crown—to the nation it was more, far more,—it was the day-spring of civil and religious freedom. It chronicles the fearful whirlwind which scattered, in awful fury before it, the stagnant and accumulated evils of ages, but which was, by its very violence, eventually to purify the land. The

---

[1] Baker's Chron. p. 232.   [2] Rich. III. act 5. scene 3.

two armies met in a large plain near the town of
Bosworth, and few conflicts were undertaken with
more determined spirit. The Earl of Richmond's
force was less than that of King Richard, but both
numbered on their sides warriors of undaunted
courage. The appearance of the Earl was greatly
in his favour; in stature he was above the common height—of great muscular strength, pleasing
countenance, and distinguished bearing.[1] He displayed the ensign of Cadwallader, the red dragon
of the native princes of Britain, to commemorate
his descent from them, and to revive the remembrance of Merlin's prophecies, and the predictions
of the great bard Taliesin. Richard in defiance
of his rival, went to the field of battle crowned
as a king. Though neither deformed nor hunch-
backed,[2] as the prejudice of party spirit has so
long delighted to portray the exterior of so un-
amiable a character, he was nevertheless pallid,
diminutive, and of repulsive aspect;[3] but his courage was invincible, his personal bravery almost
superhuman : and there hung about his speech,
his voice, and his address, a degree of fascination
that rendered him irresistible, when he was bent on
subduing men's minds to his own purposes.[4] Few
possessed so profound a knowledge of the human
heart as Richard III. He could read all its work-

[1] Bacon's Hen. VII. p. 246.　[2] See Appendix D.
[3] Sir Thos. More, p. 154.　[4] Baker's Chron. p. 234.

ings, and penetrate its weaknesses ; he knew the
effect which regal attributes, and pomp, and splendour have on the vulgar and illiterate : he also
knew his rival's personal advantages, as contrasted
with his own mean appearance ; it was not therefore merely to scorn the pretensions of Richmond,
and to grace his own cause, that in imitation of
Henry V. at Agincourt, he led his army to the
contest encircled by the kingly diadem,[1] but
chiefly with the view of impressing on his troops,
that the fate of their monarch depended on their
exertions; and glorious as were the actions of
Henry in that famous battle, he was fully equalled
by his imitator, in the prodigies of valour, which
Richard this day achieved on Bosworth field. For
a brief period the victory was doubtful, and Henry
of Richmond sent earnestly to beseech the aid of
Lord Stanley, but the recollection of his son, who
had been detained as a hostage, kept him neuter,
until near the close of the engagement. King
Richard had also commanded his presence before
the action had began, threatening the instant execution of his noble heir, in case of unnecessary
delay: but the gallant sire was callous to his
threats, as hitherto he had been proof against
his bribes. " Tell King Richard," he firmly re-
plied, " to act as it so pleaseth him—the Lord of
the Isle of Man has other sons alive !"[2]

[1] Buck's Rich. III. p. 60.   [2] Baker's Chron. 234.

Happily the Lord Strange was preserved by the same power, that willed the overthrow of King Richard. Seeking the Earl of Richmond, the enraged monarch defied him to mortal combat, and was pressing hard upon his little band, after slaying his standard-bearer, and unhorsing Sir John Cheyney,—who, seizing the banner, as it fell from Sir William Brandon's grasp, waved the British dragon in defiance—when the appearance of Lord Stanley, with his force, aided by that of his brother, Sir William Stanley, openly declaring for Henry of Tudor, decided the fate of the day.

King Richard, overpowered by numbers, was slain, and Richmond, amidst the acclamations of the whole army, was proclaimed king on the battle-field, by the title of Henry the Seventh. In the heat of the conflict, the crown had fallen from Richard's head, and was hidden by a soldier in a hawthorn bush, which, being discovered by Reginald Bray, he brought it to the Lord Stanley,[1] who, placing it on the head of his son-in-law, shouted, with enthusiasm, " Long live King Henry the Seventh !"

In remembrance of the incident, Henry caused to be erected in after years, on his superb tomb in Westminster Abbey, the device of a crown hidden in a bush, and the same scene of his rustic coronation was painted on glass, for the

[1] Harl. MSS. 542.

windows of his princely chapel, where it, to this day, remains a conspicuous and interesting object. This fierce battle, decisive as were the results, lasted but two hours, in which brief space of time was finally set at rest the contest of the Roses. By the death of Richard III. the race of the Plantagenet Kings, who had ruled the land for the space of three hundred and thirty-three years, became extinct.

Immediately after the battle, the fruits of the Lady Margaret's early lessons to her son were strikingly displayed. "The King," says the great Lord Bacon,[1] "as one that had been bred under a devout mother, and was in his nature a great observer of religious forms, caused 'Te Deum laudamus,' to be solemnly sung in the presence of the whole army upon the battle plain, where kneeling down he rendered thanks to Almighty God, for the victory he had gained."[2] After which, he commanded that all care and kindness should be paid to the wounded, then turning to the Lord of Mostyn, who had secreted him in his perilous sojourn in Wales a few months previously, he presented him with the sword and belt he had that day worn, in token of his gratitude and regard.[3]

The feeling in favour of King Henry was unani-

[1] Bacon's Hen. VII. p. 1.   [2] Baker's Chron. p. 234.
[3] Pennant's Wales, vol. i. p. 69.

mous.   By the Welsh soldiery he was viewed with superstitious reverence, because their last king, Cadwallader, had prophesied of him, as they believed, seven hundred years before—it having been revealed to him, that his offspring should again reign, again have dominion in Britain.[1] The English with scarcely less superstition, hailed in him the Prince who had long been destined to unite the Roses ;[2] and for whom they considered the Most High had fought, according to the prediction of the good King Henry the Sixth, whom they imagined to have been gifted with inspiration when testifying that the youth on whom he then looked at Eton, would gain the mastery of both factions, and win the crown for which both so vindictively fought.

Proceeding direct to Leicester from the field of battle, there is reason to infer from his making a brief stay in that city, that her son was there at length restored to the Countess of Richmond, after a separation of fourteen years—a separation marked on both sides by a series of anxieties, perils, and vicissitudes, such as are seldom compressed within so short a period, and that most rarely are apportioned to one individual.   She had parted from him a stripling, an exile, and an outlaw.   She hailed him the Monarch of England, called upon by the unanimous voice of the

[1] Baker's Chron. p. 252.   [2] Bacon's Hen. VII. p. 247.

nation to bring peace to his desolated land. From a grave and serious child, he had become a gallant and victorious Prince. It needs no other testimony but the records of their past lives to comprehend the feelings which marked the first embrace of Margaret of Lancaster and King Henry the Seventh.

Prior to his departure from Leicester, the Monarch despatched Sir Robert Willoughby to the castle of Sheriff Hutton, with directions for the Princess Elizabeth to repair with all convenient speed to London, and there to remain with the Queen Dowager, her mother, which she did with a stately retinue suited to her now elevated position, as the affianced Queen of England.[1] The King himself proceeded by slow journeys to the metropolis, amidst the unbounded acclamations of his subjects, which ardent greeting he received with a spirit of humility that completely accorded with the piety of his character. His first visit was to St. Paul's Cathedral, where he offered up the standards borne on the day of his victory, and after having heard prayers, and joined with fervent devotion in the service of the church, he adjourned to the Bishop's palace where he rested for some days.[2] Here he assembled his council, and renewed most solemnly his vow of espousing the Lady Elizabeth of York, it having

[1] Bacon's Hen. VII. p. 7.   [2] Grafton's Chron. p. 854.

been reported in Brittany, that, if successful in
gaining the English crown, the Earl of Richmond
purposed to marry the Lady Anne of Brittany,
heiress to that Duchy, and the highly gifted and
only child of Francis and the Lady Marguerite de
Foix. The affliction, which Lord Bacon says,
this report occasioned the Princess Elizabeth,[1]
greatly corroborates the testimony of Humphrey
Brereton, as relates to their private betrothment
at the period above stated; while the circumstance
of Henry the Seventh placing his bride elect under
the protection of the Queen mother, controverts
the opinion that she ever seriously entertained the
idea of making her child the consort of her own
uncle; of him, who was the reported murderer—
certainly the unblushing usurper of her son's lawful rights and realm.   The spirit of research, now
so rife, and the eager desire that prevails at this
time, of proving or disputing facts, passively received as such, merely from the long copied
relation of a few popular and oft-times prejudiced
annalists, is likely to throw a new light on innumerable occurrences connected with the Plantagenet race.   Various incidents on which from
childhood we have been accustomed to linger with
romantic delight, or to shrink from with undisguised horror and amazement, must ere long give
place to more impartial statements, and be judged

[1] Bacon's Hen. VII. p. 8.

by that calm philosophic inquiry, which can distinguish the result of mere political rumours from actual and authenticated truths.

The art of printing which has so aided to substantiate the virtues, and palliate the vices of subsequent monarchs, exercised but a feeble influence, until after the race of York had fallen from its high and palmy state; and the heated and exaggerated statements of those who sought patronage and support from the victorious Lancastrian party, were as little likely to be controverted by persons uninterested in the conquered faction, as to meet with opposition from such as risked evil to themselves by volunteering details, which it was both dangerous and fruitless to promulgate.

In compiling either historical or biographical memoirs, the actions of contemporary monarchs are comparatively unimportant, unless any leading events tend to elucidate the character or career of the eminent person under consideration. The life of the Countess of Richmond stands unparalleled in this matter, for whether viewed in its outset as the kinswoman and sister by marriage to Henry the Sixth, or at its close as the mother of Henry the Seventh,— whether jealously watched by King Edward the Fourth, as the parent of the exiled Tudor, or patronized by King Richard the Third, as

M

the consort of the powerful Stanley—her progress through life is so inseparably connected, so
absolutely interwoven with the rise and fall of
these several kings, that a brief survey of the
leading actions of their reigns, is indispensable
towards forming a just conclusion as to the extent
of her trials, and the amount of her virtues. It
has also been needed to explain any seeming in-
consistency between the profession and the practice
of one, who made religion the basis of that uncompromising integrity, which characterized Margaret of Lancaster. Having, however, minutely
traced the variety of conflicting circumstances
which ended in her son becoming the monarch
of England, it will be advisable to retreat from
public to private life, and again limit attention
to considering the Countess of Richmond in her
domestic career, lest the close of her eventful
life should be eclipsed by that illustrious personage, from whom hitherto had flowed her sorrows,
trials, and vicissitudes, but in whom, henceforth,
was to be reflected to her admiring sight, all that
maternal pride could desire, and more than human
foresight could have apprehended.

The establishment of King Henry on the throne,
appears to have been the signal to his admirable
parent for retiring from all matters connected with
public affairs. This course was adopted from the
same prudent and wise policy which induced her

ever to look more to future results than to present consequences. She well knew that her son derived but an imperfect title to the throne from her, on account of the limitation as believed of that act which alone constituted the legitimacy of her inheritance; for there can be little doubt that had Henry the Seventh been aware that the original instrument of Richard the Second had never been superseded, but merely been interlined when exemplified by Henry the Fourth, he would have grounded his right to the crown apart from his marriage with Elizabeth of York, and not have rested his title as regards himself on conquest, or his Welsh pedigree. In any case, however, the Lady Margaret could not but be conscious that his pretensions from the house of Lancaster, however lightly regarded, arose through her descent from John of Gaunt; but, she was content to see the line, of which she was the sole remaining link,* restored in the person of her offspring; she had no ambition to rule a king-

* Rymer says "There was not a prince of the house of Lancaster left in England, the preceding wars having swept them all away. Margaret of Richmond was the only person in the kingdom that could pretend any right to the crown, but even that right was far from being clear. The princes and princesses who descended from the two first marriages of John of Gaunt, chief of the Lancaster family, were all in Castile, Portugal, Germany, and the Netherlands, and did not seem inclined to assert the rights of their family." Fœdera, vol. ii. p. 2.

dom, or to assume a show of authority over its king—that king too, was the son from whom she had so long been separated, too long to have maintained any power over his opinions or actions beyond that which emanated from his cherished remembrance of early days—but he was then a dependent child—he was now a reigning monarch. Disregarding therefore all feelings of personal ambition, all claims of gratitude, all ties of consanguinity, the great, the noble Margaret, submitted with all deference to a sovereign, whose rights though now capable of being viewed in a somewhat different light, were then considered doubtful from every source but that which he least liked to admit—his union with Elizabeth of York. The Countess of Richmond never appeared at court in any other character than that of the affectionate parent she had always proved; one who set a bright example of obedience and submission to the laws of the land, without sacrificing maternal affection, or lessening that dignity which was due to her own exalted birth and singular rectitude of conduct.

The course of this narrative is now brought to the close of the year 1485. On the thirtieth of October, to ensure the fruits of his recent victory, and to render more valid his unanimous election to the throne, Henry the Seventh caused himself to be crowned at Westminster, but with that

absence of display and ostentation, which marked
all matters connected with his own merely personal
concerns. He had nearly completed his thirtieth
year, and the Countess of Richmond her forty-
sixth. Having had no issue by her second or
third husband, the son of Edmund Tudor remained her only child; but the maternal affection,
which hitherto had centred exclusively in him, was
about to be shared by another. On her son's
union with the Lady Elizabeth of York, she
welcomed her as a daughter, and treated her with
the tenderness of a parent. They were rarely
separated, and the attachment which appears from
undoubted authority to have existed between
these illustrious ladies, tends yet more to sanction
the belief of the youthful Princess having been
early associated with the Lord Stanley, and the
Lady Margaret; which latter was known to have
been most zealous in promoting her marriage with
Henry the Seventh, and thus realizing the hopes
which that connection held out of peace and con-
tentment to all parties. Previously, however, to
redeeming his pledge to the Yorkists, the King
hastened to fulfil the claims of personal gratitude
and affection. One of his earliest acts[1] naturally
was, to reverse the attainder of his mother. He
not only restored to her the lands and titles of
which she had been deprived by the disabling

[1] Rot. Parl. v. 285.

statute of Richard the Third, but he "empowered her to sue and be sued as a single woman, and to make grants, &c. as if she were unmarried.* She was dignified by the style of "the full noble Princess Margaret, Countess of Richmond, Mother of our Sovereign Lord the King;" and subsequently, by letters patent, Henry secured to her all her honours and manorial rights, notwithstanding any grants which might have been made by King Edward the Fourth, or Richard the Third.[1]

His uncle, Jasper Tudor, the faithful follower of all his fortunes, and the sharer of all his miseries, he created Duke of Bedford, and bestowed on him various places of trust and emolument.   The Lord Stanley, to whom Henry was doubly bound as his mother's husband, and as the arbiter of his own fate at Bosworth field, he elevated to the rank of Earl of Derby ; and the Baron Shaundè who had been his chosen friend in Brittany, and who it will be remembered assisted him in escaping from the insidious snare laid for him by Edward the Fourth, he made Earl of Bath.[2]   The eldest son of the unfortunate Duke of Buckingham, he restored to all his

---

* This grant gave her one of the peculiar privileges of the queen consort, who is the only person whom the law considers single.

[1] Rot. Parl. vi. 446.   [2] Baker's Chron. p. 237.

dignities and possessions.[1] Bishop Morton, whose inviolable fidelity to Henry the Sixth, had secured for him that confidence from Edward the Fourth which was so well repaid to his unhappy offspring, was constituted Lord Chancellor of the realm, and eventually advanced to the see of Canterbury.[2] Christopher Urswicke, the Lady Margaret's faithful priest, was made Dean of York, and appointed private chaplain and almoner to the King;[3] and the zealous, indefatigable, and trusty Reginald Bray was created a knight banneret, and attached to the royal person as Treasurer and Privy Counsellor.[4] Henry also issued a proclamation to the effect that all persons who would submit themselves to his government and take the oath of allegiance, should be pardoned.[5] He granted considerable immunities and privileges to the towns in Wales, which had befriended his former escape, and aided his return; and the deceased monarch Richard the Third, having been interred at Leicester without the funeral solemnities suited to his kingly rank, he caused a tomb to be made, and set over the place where he was buried, with his effigy in alabaster.[6] That monarch's remains were borne from the field of battle to the grave by his Poursuivant

[1] Bacon's Hen. VII. [2] Dugdale's Baron. ii. p. 239.
[3] Excerpta Hist. p. 109. [4] Testamenta Vetusta, p. 446.
[5] Bacon's Hen. VII. p. 14. [6] Buck's Rich. III. p. 147.

" Blanc Sanglier," so termed from his device of
the white boar, but after his interment, Henry
the Seventh changed the title of that honourable
office to " Rouge-Dragon," in commemoration of
the ancient British standard which he had conse-
crated at St. Paul's.

Having thus terminated the first year of his
reign, by satisfying his conscience and advancing
the interests of the most zealous of his friends ;
besides making many wise enactments, that
evinced his desire to temper justice with mercy,
he commenced the second year by solemnizing
his marriage with the Princess Elizabeth; an event
that was hailed with such universal and unbounded
demonstrations of joy,[1] that the dawn of 1486
teemed with brighter prospects of harmony to the
country than had illumined the political horizon
since the time that Edward the Third and the
good Queen Philippa, the progenitors of the present royal pair, had ascended the throne.

He marked this event by an act of justice to
the Queen Dowager and her royal offspring, by
reversing the statute of Richard the Third, which
had so cruelly degraded the widow and children
of Edward the Fourth.[2]   The former he restored
to her dignity, as a woman and a Queen ;[3] and by
letters patent,[4] issued shortly afterwards, he

[1] Bacon's Hen. VII. p. 16.
[2] Rot. Parl. vi. 288.   [3] Rot. Parl. vi. 289.
[4] Rot. Patent. 1 Hen. VII. p. 3. m. 25.

granted her an annuity for life, and various lordships in lieu of those that were forfeited by the statute which had divested her of title and lands.

While Henry the Seventh was thus sowing the seeds of peace and prosperity, calming angry passions, and quelling rebellious spirits, his excellent parent was occupied in those literary pursuits which had contributed to soothe the privacy of former and sorrowful years.

About the year 1472, William Caxton, the father of English typography, returned to England, and having learned the art of printing in the Low Countries, established a press in the immediate vicinity of Westminster Abbey. For some few years after his abode there, the civil wars, which embroiled the kingdom, and the disunited state of all parties, caused but little benefit to the community at large, from this wonderful and happy invention. Nevertheless, it slowly progressed; and, upon her son's elevation to the throne, the Countess of Richmond and Derby, became a zealous supporter of an art, from which it was evident such inestimable advantages might spring. She ordered new works to be printed, and patronized such as were published at the expence of Caxton and his fraternity. Wynken de Worde, his partner and contemporary, she appointed to the office of her printer,[1] and Caxton, who was an

[1] Baker's Preface to Fisher's Funeral Sermon.

author himself, dedicated to her one of his most curious performances, " The Historye of Kinge Blandhardyne and Queen Eglantyne."[1]   Among the earliest and most rare specimens of typography now extant is the translation of " Waltere Hylton's scala perfectionis," which was " englished and printed by desire of Margaret Countess of Richmond and Derby, in W. Caxton's house, by Wynken de Worde, anno Salutis 1484."

Thus did this eminent lady assemble around her persons remarkable for studious habits. Frequent mention is made in the privy purse expences of King Henry the Seventh, of the Countess of Richmond's Poet;[2] and she was ever a liberal promoter and munificent patron of learning and learned men. She encouraged the ladies about the court, to cultivate more gentle accomplishments; and that taste for literature and politeness which, in this reign, began to be appreciated, was mainly owing to the example and energy of the Lady Margaret.[3]

In September, 1486, the birth of a son and heir tended still more effectually to draw the hearts of the whole nation to the reigning monarch and his queen. The young prince was named Arthur, in honour of the renowned and ancient British King,[4] claimed as his progenitor by Henry the

---

[1] Walpole's Royal and Noble Authors.   [2] Excerpta Hist. p. 86.
[3] Russell's Essay on Women.   Bacon's Hen. VII, p. 18.
[4] Bacon's Henry VII. p. 18.

Seventh, a name peculiarly grateful to his faithful Welsh partisans, as both Merlin and their chief bard Taliesin, had prophesied that the aboriginal Britons should regain their dominion; and they believed that the prediction was now accomplished by the race of Tudor. To shew his desire, however, to conciliate all parties, the King selected the Queen Dowager to be sponsor to his grandson, and nominated the noble Earl of Derby, his mother's husband, one of the godfathers.[1]

Peace, however, is not easily restored to a long disputed realm, and early the following year the King was stopped in a tour he was making to redress grievances, and become better known to his subjects, by the insurrection of Lambert Simnel; who personated the unfortunate Earl of Warwick, son of the Duke of Clarence, the prince who was, according to popular report, drowned in a butt of Malmsey wine.

This rebellion was headed by the young Earl of Lincoln, formerly Henry's rival for the crown of England, in consequence of the decease of King Richard's son. The King dispatched messengers forthwith for the Queen and his mother, whom he consulted on all matters of importance.[2] They joined him at Kenilworth, and prompt measures were taken to suppress the insurrection. The Earl of Lincoln was slain at the battle of Stoke, and Lambert Simnel, being captured, was de-

[1] Leland's Collec. vol. iv. p. 210.   [2] Ibid.

graded to a menial situation in the royal household. Every precaution was adopted to subdue the disaffected spirit which this insurrection had roused in the land, by the attainder of the most influential of the leaders. They were, as may be judged, chiefly partisans of the House of York, and the early misfortunes of the King had rendered him peculiarly prone to suspicion and political jealousy from that quarter, the bitter persecution, and oft experienced treachery of the two last sovereigns of that dynasty having sunk too deeply in his heart ever to be effaced.*

At a very early period after his accession, Henry the Seventh, influenced by this feeling, and tenacious of all power, which appeared to emanate from the family of his persecutors, applied to Pope Innocent VIII. to confirm by an edict, the validity of

* It has been generally considered that King Henry had cause to suspect the Queen Dowager of fomenting the deception of Lambert Simnel, and that his indignation induced him to confine her for life in Bermondsey monastery at Southwark, and to confiscate all her lands and possessions. This long received, but most erroneous statement, is now wholly disproved. Nothing, indeed, can be more untrue, as is evinced by the Queen mother being named as appearing at court long after the date of her reputed disgrace, 1487, and receiving acts of personal kindness from the King, at so late a period as 1490. The fact is here noticed as being essential to retrieve the memory of Henry VII. from the unfounded accusation of undue severity to his mother-in-law, and of harshness to his meek and inoffensive Queen. Vide Leland's Collect. vol. iv. p. 249. and Rot. Patent. 5 H. VII. m. 20.

his alleged title to the empire of Britain, in virtue
of his descent from the ancient princes of the land.
This being admitted by the See of Rome, and his
claims, arising from popular election and right of
conquest, recognised by divers Acts of Parliament,[1]
he caused preparations to be made for crowning
the young Queen with great pomp in Westminster
Abbey towards the close of 1487; his dread of
being considered but nominally a king, and of the
Lancastrian pretensions appearing secondary to
those of York, having decided him in submitting
to that sacred form, singly and in his own person,
before his marriage with King Edward's heiress
could give a colour to his accession being the result of that alliance.

The precarious health of the Queen, and the
birth of his infant heir, followed by Simnel's insurrection, had delayed her coronation longer than
had been designed by her royal consort, which
created some discontent in the public mind; it
was therefore preceded and accompanied by marks
of popular favour, which contributed to render the
ceremony singularly striking and impressive.

On the arrival of their majesties in the vicinity
of the metropolis, King Henry made a public
entry into the city, where the pageants prepared
on the occasion were of so costly and magnificent
a description, that Elizabeth of York with the

[1] Rot. Parl. vi. 268—270.

Countess of Richmond and other ladies of elevated
rank, were privately placed to behold the scene,
in a house near St. Mary's hospital, Bishopsgate.[1]
The following morning the King and Queen
attended mass in St. Stephen's chapel, after which,
we are informed by Leland,[2] that "Her Majesty
kept her estate" in the parliament chamber, the
Countess of Richmond and Derby sitting on her
right hand.

The unanimity and affection which subsisted
between the king's mother and his gentle consort,
is a very leading feature in the Lady Margaret's
career. She supported the young queen on all
public occasions, and appears by the interest she
exhibited in matters of importance, to have considered her as a very daughter. During the im-
posing ceremony of the coronation, it is stated
that "the kings grace and my Lady his Moder
stood on a goodlye stage well latyzed," erected
between the pulpit and the high altar, from whence
they viewed the interesting spectacle;[3] and at
the banquet which followed in Westminster Hall,
the feast being limited to those who formed part
of the procession, Henry the Seventh, with his
illustrious parent, again viewed the scene from a
window on the left side of the building, out of
which was made a stage well latticed and

[1] Ives's Select Papers, 1773.
[2] Leland's Collect., vol. iv. p. 224.   [3] Ibid. p. 225.

" richely besene with clothes of arras, that they might prively at ther pleasur see that noble feste and service."[1] The faithful friend of the youthful queen, the noble Earl of Derby, was nominated to a more active part in the ceremonial, being appointed one of the commissioners for executing the office of High Steward of England on the day of the coronation,[2] an office he had previously filled on a similar occasion, though with far less display, to the king : for now, " attired in a riche gowne furred with sables, a marvellous riche cheyne of gold many fowldes abowte his neke, he rode before her Majestie the Queen, the trappur of his courser being right curiously wrought with the needle."[3] In no portion of her remarkable life, does the Countess of Richmond appear to greater advantage than at this period; the most exalted female in the land, next to the reigning queen, she yet acted as though she were the most lowly; consulted by her royal son on all matters of real importance, she nevertheless kept herself aloof from all obvious interference, and was so unostentatious in her demeanour, so open and upright in her dealings, that it is difficult to reconcile such extreme humility with the pride of birth and wealth in which from infancy she had been nurtured. Under the most severe dispensations

---

[1] Leland's Collect., vol. iv. p. 227.

[2] Collins' Peerage, vol. ii. p. 64. [3] Leland's Collect. p. 227.

of Providence she had remained calm and un-
moved. She never felt herself forsaken while
she had religion for her shield and support ;
but her fortitude in adversity was not greater
than her moderation in prosperity : and she so
constantly accustomed herself to witness the
sufferings of the poor and the afflicted, that gratitude for mercies vouchsafed to herself and the
object of her strongest earthly affection, preserved
her from ever being unduly elated by the smiles
of fortune.

Stow says "it would fill a volume to recount
her good deeds ;" and her biographer and confessor narrates such a series of benevolent actions,
as fully to sanction the eulogium passed on her by
Camden, who states "that the merits of the
famous Margaret Countess of Richmond and
Derby, exceeds the highest commendation that
can be given."[1] She was indeed a singular instance of genuine goodness and pure devotion, in
an age remarkable for blind and superstitious
bigotry. Performing daily and with the most
ardent zeal, all the religious offices appointed by
the church of Rome, practising the severity of its
discipline with a rigour that gave even an ascetic
cast to her piety, she nevertheless with that glad-
some spirit which seems to have shed such a
charm over her domestic life, abandoned not the

[1] Camden's Britt. vol. i. p. 337.

amusements of the court, though she scrupulously
avoided all participation in its cabals and intrigues.
From the period of her son's marriage, the Countess of Richmond added dignity, by her presence,
to his feasts, and gave confidence and support to
his meek and retiring consort, at all the pageants
which are recorded as having been celebrated
during his reign. Thus, it is mentioned that she
accompanied her majesty in state by water from
Greenwich, when invited by the mayor and civic
authorities to witness a nautical fête given by them,
the Friday previous to her coronation, where,
amongst other pageants, "well and curiously
devised, to give her highness sport and pleasure,
was a barge containing a dragon spouting flames
of fire into the Thames." [1] At an entertainment
given by the King at Windsor on St. George's
day, the Lady Margaret and her royal daughter-
in-law were present, each being habited in a gown
of the Order of the Garter." [2] At the Christmas
festivities at Shene in 1489, the Queen was attended by the Countess of Richmond and Derby,
and in the November of 1490 the king's mother
was still with her majesty, continuing her usual
attentions preparatory to the birth of her infant
daughter, [3] which took place on the 29th of that
month.

[1] Ives's Select Papers, 1773.
[2] Leland's Collect. vol. iv. p. 258.   [3] Ibid. 259.

N

The little princess was named " Margaret" after
her august grandmother, a name destined to be
of singular import in the regal annals of this kingdom ; as from the Lady Margaret of Lancaster
are descended all the kings of England who have
wielded the sceptre since the accession of her son
Henry the Seventh ; and by the union of this royal
infant, her namesake, at the age of fourteen with
James the Fourth, King of Scotland, are descended
all subsequent monarchs of that realm.   This
latter became also the ancestress of the first and
every succeeding sovereign of Great Britain, when,
on the death of her niece Queen Elizabeth of immortal memory, the two crowns were united in
the same personage, and that title adopted by King
James the First, her grandson.[1]   At the christening of the royal infant, which was performed with
great ceremony, the Countess of Richmond and
Derby stood sponsor, and presented her royal
godchild with a chest of silver gilt filled with gold,
borne by her maternal brother the Lord Welles.[2]

Prosperous, however, as seemed the opening
years of her son's reign, his peace and repose were
still embittered by great struggles, and disturbed
by unceasing cabals.   When once the spirit of
discord has taken root in a land, it is no easy matter to extirpate it, or to eradicate the baneful in-

[1] Baker's Preface to Funeral Sermon, p. vi.
[2] Leland's Collect. vol. iv. p. 238.

fluence which evil passions and malignant feelings engender. Scarcely had Henry the Seventh quelled insurrection in his native country, by the defeat and degradation of Lambert Simnell; than he was called upon to set at rest, by force of arms, or conciliatory measures, the long-protracted quarrel between France and England. Henry was sufficiently politic to perceive he could neither seize nor retain the crown of that realm;[1] he therefore accepted, as a compromise, an enormous subsidy, wherewith to enrich the impoverished coffers of the kingdom, together with a princely allowance, as a yearly payment to himself. And happy was it that he adopted so pacific a course; for the appearance of a fresh claimant for his throne, in the person of Perkin Warbeck, again involved both himself and his subjects in the misery of domestic war. This youth appeared on the arena of strife as Richard Duke of York, believed to have been murdered by Richard the Third, but now proclaimed as having been secretly preserved and educated in Flanders, where he remained concealed until he was of an age to assert his claims. The pretensions of Perkin Warbeck being sanctioned by the Duchess of Burgundy, the aunt of the missing Princes; and his alleged rights supported by a variety of stubborn facts, so startling, as to have caused almost up to the present day, a strong con-

[1] Lord Bacon's Hen. VII. p. 99.

viction that he was in truth the illustrious individual whose title he assumed, he became a formidable rival to Henry the Seventh, and a subject of great agitation to the once more divided state. All the dissatisfied remnant of the Yorkist faction thronged to the standard of the " White Rose of England," as Perkin was denominated at the court of Burgundy; where a guard of honour, clothed in murrey and blue, were appointed by the Duchess to be in attendance on his person, all deference being paid him in public and private, that was due to a prince of the blood royal of England.[1] Most of the nobler connections and adherents of the unhappy race of Plantagenet had transferred their allegiance to the Lady Elizabeth of York, when they believed her to be the legal representative of their party. Hesitation and misgivings were soon, however, apparent, as the report of the preservation of young Richard, her brother, gained ground, and obtained credence from many qualified to judge of the validity of his tale; till at length the cause of the supposed murdered Prince was openly and unhesitatingly espoused by some of the highest of the nobility, from their conviction of his being the lawful and true heir to the throne.

Henry the Seventh, though brave, was the friend of peace. He strove to maintain the power he had gained by the sword, by a wisdom which ren-

[1] Baker's Chron. p. 242.

dered him as formidable to his unruly subjects, as
dreaded by his foreign allies,—and which obtained
for him, from the great Lord Bacon, the appellation of the " Solomon of England."[1] He invariably prefaced his treaties (says that eminent
writer) by stating, " that when Christ came into
the world, peace was sung; and when He went
out of the world, peace was bequeathed. And
this vertue could not proceede out of fear, or
softness; for he was valiant and active, and therefore it was truly Christian and moral."[2] Con-
forming to his doctrine, he never unsheathed the
sword until he had tried, to the utmost, the effect
of pacificatory measures. He experienced, however, but little tranquillity, even after his treble
rights to the throne had been proclaimed by the
church, the law, and the sword, and fully confirmed by his union with the acknowledged heiress
of the long-disputed crown.

Perkin Warbeck, having been openly received
with princely honours by the King of France, and
his pretensions favourably viewed by other foreign
potentates, Henry resolved on sending agents to
the court of Burgundy, where his cause was most
triumphant, to ascertain the names of the most
powerful of his English supporters; hoping, that
by determined acts of severity towards a few of
the leaders, he might stay the misery consequent

[1] Lord Bacon's Hen. VII., p. 231. [2] Ibid. 233.

on avowed insurrection. Sir Robert Clifford, the mercenary spy and perfidious friend, betrayed the confidential intercourse of those noble minds, whose candour worked their ruin.* He headed his list of the denounced with the name of Sir William Stanley, brother to the Earl of Derby, Lord Chamberlain of the King's household, in whom Henry the Seventh had placed unbounded confidence, and whom he had distinguished with especial honour and regard, in consequence of the aid he had afforded him in conjunction with the Lord Stanley, at the battle of Bosworth. Sir William Stanley was openly arraigned as a conspirator, and, with heroic firmness, pleaded guilty to the charge of being favourably disposed to King Edward's race.[1] The result of his trial would seem to confirm the reports yet extant in many old chronicles, that he had aided the aspiring Perkin with large sums of money towards establishing his right;[2] for, on the 16th of February, 1495, this distinguished warrior was beheaded on Tower Hill. It can scarcely be ima-

---

* In the Privy Purse expences of Henry VII., proof occurs in the following entry, of the immense bribe, bestowed on Sir Robert Clifford for betraying his accomplices,—" Delivered to Sir Robert Clifford, by the hand of Master Bray, £500;"—and in reward to the person who so successfully negociated with Sir Robert Clifford, £26 13s. 4d. (Excerpta Hist. p. 86.)

[1] Seacombe's House of Stanley.

[2] Bernard Andreas, MS. p. 593.

gined that an accusation, founded on mere words, would have induced the King to forget the services of so eminent a man and to disregard his close connection with the Lord Derby and his own mother. Such severity would be wholly inconsistent with the mercy that spared Lambert Simnel's life, and the gratitude he had invariably evinced to the Stanley family. Though he had found them faithful to himself, he still knew them to have been previously warm and zealous friends of Edward the Fourth; and Sir William Stanley, from having been steward of the household to the youthful Edward the Fifth, during his abode at Ludlow, was attached, in no common degree, to the memory of the ill-fated princes. The belief, therefore, which has always, more or less, prevailed, that Perkin Warbeck was indeed Richard Duke of York,[1] as effectually rescues the memory of the brave Sir William Stanley from disloyalty and treachery, as it extenuates the act of severe justice, which the chief conspirator, and most efficient supporter of his rival, met with from the hands of his offended sovereign. The documents of this period all agree in stating, that the conflict in King Henry's mind was most acute. He delayed the arraignment of Sir William Stanley for many weeks after his accusation; but a monarch cannot evince that tenderness and mercy which is

[1] See Appendix E.

the privilege of humbler individuals; and the for-
giveness which Henry Tudor would probably have
extended, with true Christian feeling, to his former friend, though present foe, was incompatible
with the justice required from the King of England to the disturber of the peace of the realm.*
This distressing occurrence appears to have been
keenly felt by all parties. The Earl of Derby
and the Lady Margaret quitted the court, and retired to Lathom Hall, their abode in Lancashire,
where they passed many months in strict seclusion,
overwhelmed with grief at the untimely death of
so near and valued a relative.

Anxious, however, to be justified to the world,
and especially to reconcile himself with the noble
Earl, and to comfort his mother, whom Lord
Bacon tells us " he did always tenderly love and
revere," Henry the Seventh resolved on visiting
them in their retirement.

Lord Derby, apprized of the honour intended,
and aware of the King's desire privately to com-
miserate and condole with him on so severe an
affliction, made suitable preparations for receiving him with the respect due to royalty. With
all possible despatch, he beautified his seats of

* A strong proof, however, is afforded of the King's grief at
this distressing event, in his having paid the Lord Chamberlain's debts, and causing him to be interred at Syon, at his own
charge.—(Excerpta Hist. p. 100.)

Lathom and Knowsley, enlarging the latter considerably, for the better accommodation of the King and his suite, who would there rest prior to their arrival at Lathom. Remembering also that there was no certain or continual passage over the river Mersey, he built a bridge, and threw up a causeway across the marshes to the rising ground on the Cheshire side, that the King might pursue his progress to the demesne of his illustrious relatives, without delay or hazard.[1]

On the 24th of June, 1495, Henry the Seventh and his Queen arrived at Knowsley Place, and from thence proceeded in state to Lathom Hall, where they sojourned about a month, with the Lord Derby and the Lady Margaret, quitting their hospitable castle well satisfied with their reception.

We are too apt to imagine, judging by the standard of human policy, that all that can render life desirable is concentrated in wealth, titles, and exalted rank. Here again the study of history, by spreading before us, as in a map, the full career of princes, nobles, and chieftains—by pourtraying their public triumphs, and making known their domestic trials, enables us to form a truer estimate of things; and to perceive how far more equally the blessings of life are distributed, than the yearning after earthly preferment allows many on a cursory

[1] Seacombe's Hist. of House of Stanley.

view to admit. The enormous wealth of Sir William Stanley—for he "was the richest subject for value in the kingdom,"—and his proud station as chamberlain and counsellor to the king, were in all likelihood the ultimate causes of his untimely death: the one aggravating his offence with his sovereign, the other being a chief incentive to the rebels to seek the enlistment of so powerful a supporter. It is indeed scarcely possible to survey the scene just narrated, without pausing to observe how painfully the duties incident on their elevated position warred with the kindly feelings of all the distinguished personages connected with the tragedy of Sir William Stanley's execution.

The King, as testified by Lord Bacon, was a " merciful prince. In twenty-four years reign," says that eminent philosopher, " though his times were full of conspiracies and troubles, he never put down, or discomposed counsellor or near servant, save only Stanley the Lord Chamberlain;" and he was the man to whom he had committed the trust of his person — whose brother had espoused his exemplary and illustrious parent, who was "no ways discontented, no ways suspected;" and who had enjoyed his favour and advancement both in honor and riches, yet he was false to him! and to a prince so sensitive, and who had been so often betrayed by friend and foe, bitter indeed must have been the conviction."

Nevertheless it is affirmed that for six weeks the
king did stay the execution, in hope of intercession; and had the Lady Margaret yielded to
the humane and gentler feelings which ever
marked her private character, there can exist
little doubt that she would have pleaded at the
foot of the throne for Stanley's brother! But
Margaret of Lancaster had stern duties to fulfil
to the country at large, that militated against
the exercise of the mild virtues that adorned the
domestic career of the Countess of Derby. She
had witnessed and bemoaned the misery of civil
discord. She had laboured unceasingly to bring
peace to the distracted land, and she wisely repressed the emotions of a wife and a kinswoman,
from the conviction that justice must be dispensed
with the same measure alike to the rich conspirator, as to the poor and friendless rebel. But that
it was a deep and bitter affliction, is evident from
the words of the same noble statesman whose
authority has been so often quoted. Lord Bacon
expressly mentions in describing the visit to Lathom, that the king "went in progresse to *comfort*
his mother, whom he did always tenderly love and
revere, and to make demonstration that the proceedings imposed upon him by necessity of state
had not in any degree diminished the affection he
bore to the noble earl his father-in-law." Thus
must all reflective minds feel that temptation

awaits us in proportion to our prosperity, and that
the path of duty is not steadily pursued even by
the most conscientious, without many a painful
conviction that it must often war with earthly
affections, yet ever be unhesitatingly pursued as
a pledge of our solemn belief that man's intentions, as well as his deeds, are registered in heaven.

A flourishing and increasing family shed over
the domestic circle of Henry the Seventh and
Elizabeth of York, that repose which party
spirit and continual insurrection had denied
to their public lives.   In addition to another
daughter, a second son had been born to them,
the noble Prince Henry, who was created at this
important crisis, Duke of York, a title that must
have been as grateful to the queen's party, as it
evinced policy and good feeling on the king's side;
to endeavour to mitigate, by means of the names
and titles of his children, those prejudices and
contending feelings that the union of the two factions in the person of himself and his royal consort
had softened, but not entirely subdued.   By the
British appellation of Arthur, bestowed on the
Prince of Wales, he bound himself, as · has
been already noticed, more firmly to his faithful
Welsh, though he counteracted all appearance of
triumph on the Lancastrian side, by selecting for
his first born, sponsors, chosen from the Yorkists,
in the persons of the Dowager Queen, and the

noble Earl of Derby. His eldest daughter
Margaret, (as also previously stated) was by
name and spiritual adoption peculiarly the child
of his own revered parent. The infant Elizabeth was called after her royal mother and
grandmother, whilst his name of Henry revived
anew in the Lancastrians the glorious days of his
progenitors, and yet rekindled by the title of Duke
of York that deep-rooted affection to the fallen
dynasty, which induced rebellion in many a generous heart, and rankled deeply in some of the
finest spirits that yielded obeisance to Henry
Tudor, merely as the husband of Elizabeth of York.

Of all materials for biography, letters are perhaps the most interesting, certainly the most
satisfactory. After the lapse of centuries, no information respecting the feelings and character of
individuals can be relied upon with greater safety;
for in their confidential correspondence, they appear, as it were, before us in their own persons,
and exhibit their thoughts and attainments in
true and natural colours. Though unfortunately
only a few of the Countess of Richmond's letters
are preserved, they are such authentic relics, that
they could not with propriety be omitted in a
memoir of her life; more especially as the earliest
now extant[1] shows the Countess's affection for her

[1] The original is in the Tower, and printed literally in the
Excerpta Historica, p. 285.

son, for the queen, and for her grandchildren, in a peculiarly pleasing and unaffected manner. It was addressed to the Earl of Ormond, the Queen's chamberlain, apparently during his embassy[1] to France, towards the end of 1495 or early in 1496.

"MY LORD CHAMBERLAIN,

" I thank you heartily that ye list so soon remember me with my gloves, the which were right good, save they were too much for my hand. I think the ladies in that parts be great ladies all, and according to their great estate they have great personages. As for news here I am sure ye shall have more surety than I can send you. Blessed be God, the King, the Queen, and all our sweet children be in good health. The Queen hath been a little crased, but now she is well, God be thanked. Her sickness is so good as I would but I trust hastily it shall, with God's grace,[*] whom I pray give you good speed in your great matters, and bring you well and soon home.

" Written at Shene the 25th day of April,

" M. RYCHEMOND.

" To my Lord the Queen's Chamberlain."

[1] Lodge's Irish Peerage, vol. ii. p. 13.

[*] The import seems that the Queen had been ill, but the Countess hoped would soon be quite restored.

In the Spring of 1498, the Lady Margaret was again summoned by her son as sponsor to another grandchild,[1] a third prince being born at Greenwich in the fourteenth year of King Henry's reign, who was christened Edmund Tudor, in memory of his grandfather, the Earl of Richmond. The venerable Countess, now advancing in years, held the noble infant at the font,[2] while bestowing on him an appellation so fraught with conflicting feelings. Her royal god-child, in further commemoration of his grandmother's birth and descent, was created Duke of Somerset; but the little prince lived not long enough to appreciate the tenderness she early testified for the infant inheritor of such endearing appellations. He died in childhood at Bishop's Hatfield, the manor, it will be recollected, of his ancestress, Queen Katherine, and which was then the nursery of the King's children.[3] This instance of attachment to associations connected with his early days and those of his parents, was not the only proof evinced by the King of the deep respect he entertained for all that related to them. The ancient palace at Sheen, in Surry, which had witnessed such frequent festivities in his time and in that of his predecessors, he rebuilt in the sixteenth year of his reign, and changed its

[1] Sandford's Gen. Hist. Book vi. chap. 10.
[2] Leland's Collect. vol. iv. p. 243.   [3] Anglorum Spec. p. 398.

penance. She had engaged as her confessor, a
divine of eminent piety. The ascetic severities,
the fervent devotion, and unbounded charity of
John Fisher, the friend and companion of Erasmus, having come to the knowledge of the Lady
Margaret, she solicited him to quit his studies
at Cambridge and to become her spiritual guide,
and the almoner and distributor of her charities. [1]
It does not however appear, that she ever formally
embraced a conventual life, or became an inmate
of any monastic establishment, but she was admitted a member of the fraternity of five religious
houses, Westminster, Crowland, Durham, Wyn-
burne and the Charter House, London, which
her biographer observes, " As it entitled her to
the prayers, so it gave her a share in the merits
and good works of all those holy societies." [2]

It is probably from her connection with these
sanctuaries purely set apart for religious duties,
that the Lady Margaret is usually represented in
the habit of a recluse ; especially as about this
time in conformity with her resolution of retiring
from the world, she solicited and obtained the
consent of the Earl of Derby, or rather,—as expressed by Bishop Fisher, " She obtained licence
in her husband's days long time before he died," [3]
for a formal separation.   According to the

[1] Coleridge's Worthies of Yorkshire.
[2] Baker's preface to Funeral Sermon. [3] Funeral Sermon, p. 11.

and evil, so fraught with wondrous changes, ought to be wholly devoted to that great and merciful Being who had never forsaken her in sorrow or in joy. It was not unusual at the era in which she flourished for persons advancing in years to procure by purchase or gift, a retreat in some holy asylum, where, abandoning earthly cares, they could devote the decline of life to prayer and confession. * Some of pure and unspotted lives, adopted such devotional retirement, from the pious wish of ending their days in a sanctuary set apart for religion, where they might be free from worldly temptations, and estranged from worldly thoughts. Others undertook it as an atonement for their former evil deeds, hoping it might ensure their pardon and secure their eternal peace;[1] and a few embraced it from love of literature, for it must not be forgotten that the great majority of people could obtain books in convents alone. The Countess of Richmond had long been preparing herself for seclusion from the pleasures and fascinations of the court, by increased severity in personal mortifications and a more rigid exercise of austere

* Cicely Duchess of York, the mother of King Edward IV. and Richard III. widow of the Duke of York who was slain at Wakefield, and grandmother of the reigning queen, became a Benedictine Nun in 1480. (Cott. MSS. Vitellius, c. 17. p. 250.)

[1] Paston Letters, vol. iv.

quit the life of retirement which she had voluntarily chosen at this period. The religious zeal
which induced seclusion from a court where her
dignified conduct had at once elevated her own
character, and that of her sex, was marked by an
increase of benevolence and charitable actions.
She supported under her roof twelve poor or
afflicted persons, whose wounds she would dress
with her own hands, and supply their wants with
the most gentle and tender piety. It was her
custom to be present at their decease, and she
generally attended their obsequies, observing that
such scenes taught her how to die.

With the ascetic spirit which marked that era
the Lady Margaret increased her personal mortifications, when thus striving to enlarge the comforts
of those around her. She would wear next her
skin, lacerating girdles and garments of hair cloth;
and withal was so strict in her devotional exercises
that her bodily health was frequently injured by
her spiritual zeal.

Dr. Fisher became a member of her household,
and in conjunction with Dr. Hornby, who was
chancellor of her court or family,[1] directed all
things therein with the austere ceremonial, and
almost rigid sanctity belonging to the monastic
orders. This excellent divine is said to have directed the studies and superintended the education of

[1] Baker's Preface to Funeral Sermon, p. 50.

the young prince, afterwards Henry the Eighth,
and the circumstance appears credible, not merely
from the proficiency of this monarch in scholastic
divinity, but because he is known to have been in
a great degree brought up by his grandmother,
and to have imbibed from her tuition and love of
literature, that taste for letters so early and strikingly displayed. This fact has been handed
down by means of an inscription in the north
aisle of the parish church of Bletshoe, on a monument to the memory of Sir John St. John,[1]
nephew of the Countess of Richmond, who it is
there stated was educated by this eminent lady
together with her grandson Prince Henry ; who
retained for his youthful associate in study and
amusement so strong a regard, that in after years
when Monarch of England, he made St. John
guardian of his daughters Mary and Elizabeth
the future queens. He died in the office of
chamberlain to the latter, and the effigy of a
knight in armour, together with the before-men-
tioned inscription, commemorates this distinguished
ancestor of the barons St. John of Bletshoe, and
the Viscounts Bolingbroke ; which last title was
bestowed on account of the connection of their
progenitors with the Lady Margaret of Lancaster.[2] The nurture and tuition of her young kins-
folk is a further instance of the extent to which

[1] Lyson's Mag. Brit.   [2] Camden's Brit. vol. i. p. 337.

the countess cherished the claims of consanguinity, and how beautifully she blended the
moral virtues with the extreme of devotional enthusiasm, even to the latest hour of her life. The
young St. John, who had shared with her royal
grandson, the tenderness of her love, and benefited by the value of her precepts; she appointed
in maturer years, chamberlain of her household,
and left him one of the executors of her will.
She as zealously promoted the interests of a
younger half-brother, by the Duchess of Somerset's third marriage, John Lord Wells, who was
created a viscount by her son Henry the Seventh; [1]
and by his union with the Princess Cicely the
queen's sister, was intimately associated with herself
and the royal family. This nobleman dying without
heirs in 1498, the title became extinct.

About this period Lady Margaret completed the
superb altar tomb to the memory of her noble parents in Wimborne Minster, and augmented a
chauntry previously established by one of the early
monarchs, wherein she ordained mass to be daily
celebrated, for the souls of herself, of her son
Henry the Seventh, of her parents and her ancestors; the collects and other ceremonies being particularly specified. She founded likewise a free
school at Wimborne, and procured letters patent
from her son for its endowment, bequeathing an

[1] Camden's Brit. vol. i. p. 567.

annual stipend to a priest to teach grammar free
to all who should demand it, according to the custom of the schools of Eton and Winchester; en-
joining the residence of the chaplain in a house set
apart for that purpose, and forbidding all perqui-
sites from the scholars, or any fees but such as were
derived from her endowment. This fine institution yet exists, but from having been considerably
enlarged and benefited by letters patent granted
by Queen Elizabeth her great-grand-daughter, its
original appellation was altered from that of "the
Lady Margaret's," to Queen Elizabeth's free
Grammar School.[1]

Peaceably occupied with undertakings such as
these, and in planning various other great and
good deeds, tending to advance true piety and
encourage that growth of knowledge which
springing in great measure from the seeds she
scattered and sowed in a barren soil, has since
attained to such a height as now to overshadow
with its branches our highly favoured land; it is
necessary to leave the venerable countess pursuing her tranquil and enlightened path, to perceive
by another brief glance at the state of public
affairs, how peculiarly valuable were her single
efforts to effect in the minds of the rising generation a more civilized and peaceable feeling than
that turbulent and factious spirit which yet held

[1] Hutchinson's Dorset, Art. Wimborne.

in thraldom the mass of King Henry's rebellious
subjects.

The insurrection which led to the execution of
Sir William Stanley was not quelled by his death
or by the rigorous measures taken by Henry to
crush the rebellion at its commencement. For
the space of five years both the king and the
country were harassed with civil war, and once
more a prey to cabal, to executions, and to
attainder. Sometimes as a leader of a successful
band, at others a wanderer in foreign courts,
Perkin Warbeck contrived to keep England,
Scotland, and Ireland, in a state of continual
agitation. Having at length been taken prisoner,
Henry spared his life, under a promise of submission to close imprisonment in the Tower, but
being speedily found to be planning his escape,
in conjunction with the unfortunate Earl of Warwick, who had been a captive from the period of
his father's execution in the reign of Edward IV.
he was tried for high treason, and beheaded at
Tyburn, in November 1499, the unhappy prince
his associate undergoing the same fate on Tower
Hill a few weeks after, in the 24th year of his
age. By this tragical event, the rebellion was
repressed, [1] though the fate of the persecuted
Warwick will ever remain a blot on the escutscheon
of the three monarchs, who, without the shadow

[1] Excerpta Hist. p. 123.

of cause beyond that inspired by jealousy and
mistrust, held him in captivity, from the days of
his childhood, until he terminated his melancholy
life, by the premature and violent death which in
some form or other befel all who bore the name
of Plantagenet, of which he was the last male
descendant. But though peace was restored to
the land by Perkin Warbeck's execution, prosperity was by no means the result. Towards the
close of the same year, the plague made its appearance with fearful malignity, completing the
desolation that the sword had begun. Henry the
Seventh and his queen, after many change of
places, were obliged to fly to Calais to avoid its
effects, thirty thousand persons having become
victims to its fury in the city of London alone.[1]

In the year 1500, her Majesty presented the
nation with another Princess, the Lady Mary,[*]
through whom the House of Stanley subsequently
became allied by blood as well as by marriage, to
the illustrious subject of this memoir ; Margaret,
grand-daughter of the Princess Mary, having
espoused Henry fourth Earl of Derby.[2] This

[1] Bacon's Hen. VII. p. 196.

[*] Grandmother of the unfortunate Lady Jane Grey. The
sisters of this lamented lady, are likewise subjects of great
historical interest, especially Lady Katherine Grey, who is
here noticed from having been committed to the custody of
Sir Thomas Gresham.

[2] See Appendix G.

event was soon followed by the marriage of Arthur, Prince of Wales, with the Princess Katherine, the daughter of Ferdinand, and Isabella of
Spain. She was a descendant of John of Gaunt's
daughter, by Dōna Constantia of Castille, and was
consequently connected with the House of Lancaster, and the rejoicings which took place on the
occasion prove the general satisfaction felt at the
alliance, for they stand unrivalled, in our festive
records, for splendour and magnificence; we might
likewise add, also for singularity. Unless authentic
documents had been preserved, it would scarcely
enter into the imagination to conceive such an
extraordinary exhibition; or to comprehend the
possibility of so incongruous a mixture of puerile
devices and miscalled religious display. Excepting that in an historical memoir, all digressions
that tend to elucidate the manners and customs of
the age, are admissible—nay, essential to the just
comprehension of the position of the individual
whose career it records, it would scarcely seem
within the province of this narrative to describe
any of the ceremonies observed on this occasion;
but, as "the Venerable Margaret" was induced to
leave the religious seclusion she had chosen, to
witness that portion of the festivity *esteemed devotional,* and as she farther evinced her gratifica-
tion at the alliance, by entertaining the Lord
Mayor and civic authorities at Cold Harbour,

which was her temporary city residence ;[1] it may
not be considered irrelevant or altogether uninteresting to state, that the entrance of the Princess
Katherine into London was celebrated amongst
innumerable other testimonies of public rejoicing,
by the display of a succession of pageants, along
the line of procession from London Bridge to St.
Paul's Church Yard.

The first of these dramatic exhibitions was a
representation of the Holy Trinity, surmounted by
angels offering incense, and supported by St.
Catherine and St. Ursula, who addressed the
Princess, in long poetical propositions, on her
reaching London Bridge. The second pageant
exhibited the insignia of the royal family, under
the device of a huge castle, above which towered
a ponderous portcullis—a fearful red dragon with
a crown of gold, and gigantic red roses, half a
yard in breadth : in this show, called the " Castle
of Portculleys," two knights and a bishop under
the names of Policy, Nobleness, and Virtue, delivered long harangues. The third exhibition was
that of the Moon, with extravagant representations
of the starry firmament, in which the bride was
compared to Hesperus, and Prince Arthur to
Arcturus : above this sphere sat the angel Ra-
phael, who also delivered a long proposition in
verse, as did characters representing Alphonso

[1] Wilkinson's Lond. illustrata.

King of Spain (the famed ancestor of the
Princess), the prophet Job, and Boethius. The
fourth pageant was that of the Sun, typical of the
bridegroom, with equally outrageous accompani-
ments ; for in all the devices there was a great
share of astronomy—a belief in fortunes told from
the stars being one of the superstitions of the age.
The fifth was called the Temple of God, which
with singular profaneness represented " the God-
head" surrounded by innumerable angels, and supported by the four Evangelists, and at this pageant
the Princess heard a poetical sermon, presumed to
be delivered by the ALMIGHTY himself !¹ To this
same spot the King also had privately repaired,
attended by Prince Arthur, the Earl of Derby, and
others of the court ; and, in a merchant's chamber adjoining, though concealed from general observation, stood the Queen, the young Princesses
Margaret and Mary, and the Countess of Richmond and Derby, who is said to have " wept marvellously at the great triumph of the marriage, in
drede that some adversyte might follow.'"² How
saddening is it to reflect on the low state of taste
and feeling, that could have made kings, prelates,
chieftains, and scholars, take part in and feel

¹ Abridged from a MS. in the College of Arms, printed in
the Antiquarian Repertory. See also Bacon's Henry VII.,
p. 205.
² Fisher's Funeral Sermon, p. 31.

profited by such a mixture of the awful and absurd.

Perverted, indeed, must have been the purity of religion, when, by performances such as these, the fearful mysteries of Heaven could presumptuously be attempted to be portrayed by man. From so melancholy a picture, it is cheering to observe how pure must have been the faith, how exemplary the practice of the Lady Margaret, when her pious deeds and munificent acts were of so exalted and truly Christian a character as to be no less admirable at the present time than in those days of false devotion in which she flourished.

The most interesting part of the Countess of Richmond's correspondence seems to belong to this period; but the only letter of which the date can positively be ascertained, was one written on Saint Anne's day, July 26th, 1501, apparently the latest extant. Throughout the whole, her tenderness and love for her son is most striking, and her endearing expressions fully prove the harmony and affection that existed between them.

The claim upon the King of France, so often alluded to, was for money advanced by the Duchess of Somerset — the Lady Margaret's mother,—to the Duke of Orleans, while that Prince was a prisoner in this country; and her right to which, it is shewn, by the following letter,[1] she had wholly yielded to her son.

" My own sweet and most dear King, and all my worldly joy.

" In as humble manner as I can think, I recommend me to your grace, and most heartily beseech our Lord to bless you. And my good heart, where that you say that the French King hath at this time given me courteous answer, and written letter of favour to his Court of Parliament, for the brief expedition of my matter, which so long hath hanged; the which I well know he doth especially for your sake, for the which my ....ly beseech your Grace it............to give him your favourable......... thanks, and to desire hiim to continue his...... in...e...... me. And, if it so might like your Grace, to do the same to the cardinal ; which, as I understood, is your faithful, true, and loving servant. I wish my very joy, as I oft have shewed, and I fortune to get this, or any part thereof, there shall neither be that or any good I have, but it shall be your's, and at your commandment, as surely and with as

---

[1] From the original in the Cottonian MSS. Vespasian F. xiii. fo. 60 ;—where there is also preserved an order from the Countess of Richmond to Richard Shirley, her bailiff, commanding him to provide provisions against the arrival of the King at her town of Ware. Written at the manor of Hatfield, the 23rd day of July (Ibid. fo. 61.)

good a will, as any ye have in your coffers; and would God ye could know it, as verily as I think it. But, my dear heart, I will no more encumber your Grace with further writing in this matter, for I am sure your chaplain and servant, Dr. Whytston, hath shewed your highness the circumstances of the same; and if it so may please your Grace, I humbly beseech the same, to give further credence also to this bearer. And our Lord give you as long good life, health, and joy, as your most noble heart can desire, with as hearty blessings as our Lord hath given me power to give you.

" At *Colyweston the 14th day of January, by your faithful, true bedewoman[1] and humble mother,

" MARGARET R."[2]

The annexed letter from King Henry the

* Colyweston, in Northamptonshire, from whence the above letter is dated, was the favourite residence and frequent abode of the Lady Margaret. The mansion she there erected was noticed, early in this memoir; an entry is twice made in the Privy Purse expences of King Henry VII. of his visit to it; and Leland states, that this dwelling of her venerable grandmother was selected as the state resting place of the Princess Margaret, when on her progress to espouse James the IV. King of Scotland.

[1] A bedewoman was a person employed in praying; though generally it implied one who prayed for another. (Paston's letters, vol. iii. p. 254.)

[2] The signature of this letter was the one selected for the autograph prefixed to the frontispiece of this memoir.

Seventh to his mother,[1] shews that her tenderness
was repaid by a degree of filial love and venera-
tion rarely exceeded, and which at once bears
touching testimony to her worth, and redeems
many harsh traits in the character attributed to that
monarch by historians.

" Madam, my most entirely well-beloved lady
and mother.

" I recommend me unto you in the most
humble and lowly wise that I can, beseeching
you of your daily and continual blessings.   By
your confessor the bearer, I have received your
good and most loving writing, and by the same,
have heard at good leisure such credence as
he would shew unto me on your behalf, and
thereupon have sped him in every behalf without
delay, according to your noble petition and desire
which resteth in two principal points ; the one for
a general pardon for all manner causes ; the other
is for to alter and change part of a licence which
I had given unto you before, for to be put into
mortmain at Westminster, and now to be converted into the University of Cambridge for your
soul's health, etc.*   All which things according to
your desire and pleasure, I have with all my heart

[1] Harl. MS. 7039. fol. 34. from the Archives of St. John's
College of Cambridge.

* This letter first regards Christ's College, and afterwards
St. John's. (Baker's Appendix to Funeral Sermon, p. 40.)

and good-will given and granted unto you. And
my Dame, not only in this but in all other things
that I may know should be to your honour and
pleasure, and weal of your soul, I shall be as glad
to please you as your heart can desire it, and I
know well that I am as much bounden so to do as
any creature living, for the great and singular
motherly love and affection that it hath pleased
you at all times to bear towards me. Wherefore,
my own most loving mother, in my most hearty manner I thank you, beseeching you of your good con-
tinuance in the same. And, Madam, your said
confessor, hath moreover shewn unto me on your
behalf, that ye of your goodness and kind disposition, have given and granted unto me such
title and interest as ye have or ought to have in
such debts and duties which is owing and due
unto you in France, by the French king and
others ; wherefore, Madam, in my most hearty and
humble wise I thank you. Howbeit, I verily
think it will be right hard to recover it without it
be driven by compulsion and force, rather than
by any true justice, which is not yet as we think
any convenient time to be put in execution.

"Nevertheless it hath pleased you to give us a
good interest and mean, if they will not conform
them to reason and good justice, to defend or offend at a convenient time when the case shall so
require hereafter. For such a chance may fall

that this your grant might stand in great stead for
a recovery of our right, and to make us free,
whereas we be now bound, etc. And verily,
Madam, and I might recover it at this time or
any other, ye be sure ye should have your pleasure
therein, as I and all that God has given me, is
and shall ever be at your will and commandment,
as I have instructed Master Fisher more largely
herein, as I doubt not but he will declare unto
you. And I beseech you to send me your mind
and pleasure in the same, which I shall be full
glad to follow with God's grace, which send and
give unto you the full accomplishment of all your
noble and virtuous desires. Written at Greenwich, the 17th day of July, with the hand of your
most humble and loving son.

H. R.

After the writing of this letter, your confessor
delivered unto me such letters and writings obli-
gatory of your duties in France, which it hath
pleased you to send unto me, which I have
received by an indenture of every parcel of the
same. Wherefore, eftsoons, in my most humble
wise, I thank you, and I purpose hereafter, at
better leisure, to know your mind and pleasure
further therein. Madam, I have encumbered you
now with this my long writings, but, methinks,
that I can do no less, considering that is so seldom
that I do write, wherefore, I beseech you to

pardon me, for verily, Madam, my sight is nothing so perfect as it has been ; and I know well it will impair daily ; wherefore, I trust that you will not be displeased though I write not so often with my own hand, for on my faith, I have been three days or I could make an end of this letter."

" To my Lady."

It is evident from the date of the following letter,[1] July 26th, 1501, that the Countess of Richmond was then at Calais; but her reason for going there is not known. The conclusion shows that her son, King Henry the Seventh, was born on the 26th of July, and it is the only authority for that fact.

" My dearest, and only desired joy in this world :—

With my most hearty loving blessings, and humble commendations, I pray our Lord to reward and thank your Grace, for that it hath pleased your Highness so kindly and lovingly to be content to write your letters of thanks to the French King for my great matter that so long hath been in suit, as Master Welby hath shewed me your bounteous goodness is pleased.

" I wish, my dear heart, and my fortune be to

---

[1] Printed in Dr. Howard's collection of Letters, vol. i, p. 155.

recover it, I trust ye shall well perceive I shall
deal towards you as a kind loving mother ; and if
I should never have it, yet your kind dealing is
to me a thousand times more than all that good I
can recover, and all the French King's might be
mine withal. My dear heart, and it may please
your Highness to license Master Whitstongs for
this time to present your honourable letters, and
begin the process of my cause ; for that he so
well knoweth the matter, and also brought me the
writings from the said French King, with his
other letters to his parliament at Paris, it should
be greatly to my help, as I think ; but all will I
remit to your pleasure ; and if I be too bold in
this, or any of my desires, I humbly beseech your
grace of pardon, and that your Highness take no
displeasure.

" My good King, I have now sent a servant of
mine into Kendall, to receive such annuities as be
yet hanging upon the account of Sir William
Wall, my lord's[1] chaplain, whom I have clearly
discharged ; and if it will please your Majesty's
own heart, at your leisure, to send me a letter,
and command me that I suffer none of my tenants
be retained with no man, but that they be kept for
my Lord of York,[2] your fair sweet son, for whom

[1] The Earl of Derby.

[2] Her grandson Henry, Duke of York, afterwards King
Henry the Eighth.

they be most meet, it shall be a good excuse for
me to my lord and husband ; and then I may
well, and without displeasure, cause them all
to be sworn, the which shall not after be long
undone. And where your Grace showed your
pleasure for . . . . the bastard of King
Edward's ;[1] Sir, there is neither that, or any other
thing I may do by your commandment, but I
shall be glad to fulfil to my little power, with
God's grace.

"And, my sweet King, Fielding, this bearer,
hath prayed me to beseech you to be his good
lord in a matter he sueth for to the Bishop of
Ely, (now, as we hear, elect,[2]) for a little office
nigh to London. Verily, my King, he is a good
and a wise well-ruled gentleman, and full truly
hath served you, well accompanied, as well at
your first as all other occasions ; and that causeth
us to be the more bold, and gladder also to speak
for him ; howbeit, my Lord Marquis[3] hath been
very low to him in times past, because he would
not be retained with him ; and truly, my good
King, he helpeth me right well in such matters

[1] Sir Arthur Plantagenet, afterwards created Viscount
L'Isle.

[2] Richard Redman, Bishop of Exeter, who was translated to
Ely, in September, 1501. This fixes the date of the letter.
Bishop Alcock, the former bishop of Ely, died in October,
1500.

[3] The Marquess of Dorset.

as I have business within these parts. And, my dear heart, I now beseech you of pardon of my long and tedious writing, and pray Almighty God to give you as long, good and prosperous life as ever had Prince ; and as hearty blessings as I can ask of God.

"At Calais town, this day of Saint Anne's, that I did bring into this world, my good and gracious Prince, King, and only beloved son, by

"Your humble Servant, Bedewoman,

and Mother,

"Margaret R."

The celebrated Hugh Oldham, (the friend of Erasmus, and of the learned Dean Colet, founder of St. Paul's school,) was at this time chaplain to the Countess of Richmond ; and by her held in great favour, from his zeal in the cause of religion, and his efforts for the advancement of literature. She had presented him to the living of Swynested, in the diocese of Lincoln, and through her interest he was eventually advanced to the See of Exeter.*

* This eminent prelate was the joint founder, with Richard Fox, Bishop of Winchester, of Corpus Christi College, Oxford, which they endowed with great revenues. He strenuously promoted the instruction of youth in good and useful learning, and founded and endowed a school at Manchester. Bishop Oldham was remarkable in Ecclesiastical History for his zeal in defending the liberties and prerogatives of the church. Being under sentence of excommunication, at his death his

She was likewise the friend and early patron of William Smyth, afterwards Bishop of Lincoln, and founder of Brasen-nose College, Oxford. He was educated in her household, with many other scholars of future eminence; this illustrious lady having in this manner liberally provided for the instruction of young men of promising talents though limited means.

In the 18th year of her son's reign, the Countess of Richmond instituted two perpetual public lectures in divinity, one at Cambridge, and the other at Oxford, endowing each with twenty marks a year, now equivalent to £1000. Dr. John Fisher was appointed her first reader at the former university, which office was shortly after filled by the learned Erasmus; but although both these great benefactions bear the date of their final endowment, in 1502, it is evident that her intention, as regards Oxford, was formed at a much earlier period; for in the list of her divinity professors, given by Baker, in his preface to her funeral sermon, it seems that Edward Willesford (her confessor, after the elevation of Urswicke) read her lecture to the University of Oxford before his settlement in 1497.

body was not suffered to be interred, but absolution being procured from Rome, he was at length buried in his cathedral at Exeter, where his monument yet remains, it having been repaired in the year 1763 by the Provost and Fellows of Corpus Christi, from gratitude to their liberal benefactor.

In this year, the Lady Margaret founded a chauntry in St. George's Chapel at Windsor, for four chaplains to pray for her soul, the soul of her parents, and all faithful souls.

In 1503 she instituted a perpetual public preachership at Cambridge, with a salary of ten pounds per annum; the duty required was six sermons at least, to be delivered yearly at several churches specified in London, Ely, and Lincoln. The foundation, by royal dispensation,[1] is now altered from six sermons in different dioceses, to the same number annually delivered in the University of Cambridge at the beginning of Easter Term; so that, to quote the words of the above named able commentator of her collegiate benefactions, "this excellent lady, having taught the ignorant whilst such instruction was wanting, the world being now wiser, she instructs the learned both in the pulpit and the chair."

The marriage festivities, recently spoken of, were soon to be succeeded by the awful solemnities of death; a visitation peculiarly appalling when it falls on the first-born of a monarch, the heir-apparent to a throne. Prince Arthur survived his union with Katherine of Spain but five months. He was sent into Wales with a splendid court, to devote his time and attention to the wants and wishes of the principality from whence he derived

[1] Black Book of the University, p. 118.

his title; but consumption soon laid prostrate
the hopes that had prematurely been raised, both
in the minds of his family and his followers, from
his singularly amiable disposition, and estimable
qualities. He expired at Ludlow Castle before
he had attained his sixteenth year, to the great sorrow of the nation generally, but especially of the
Welsh, who had ever superstitiously viewed him
as " their long-lost Arthur."

The demise of the Prince of Wales was shortly
succeeded by that of his amiable mother, the royal
Elizabeth of York, who died in giving birth to a
daughter, the Princess Katherine, in the Tower of
London, the 11th of February, 1503.

The Queen was universally beloved for the
kindness of her nature, the gentleness of her character, and for that spirit of forbearance and resignation, which, throughout a life of singular trial
and difficulty, had won the admiration of her foes,
and secured the love and attachment of her friends.
She expired on the anniversary of her own birth,
at the early age of thirty-seven.   Sadness over-
spread the land, and grief was visible in every
countenance.   Pageants and feasts, which had
gradually roused a kindlier spirit in the long disunited realm, were now exchanged for funeral
obsequies, equally felt, and equally shared by both
factions.

About this time, and probably occasioned by

these afflicting events, the venerable parent of
Henry the Seventh was commanded to draw up orders, yet extant in the Heralds' College, for " great
estates of ladies and noble women," relative to
their precedence, reformation of apparel, and
sumptuary regulations at the time of mourning.[1]

The studious habits so early displayed by the
Lady Margaret constituted the great charm of
her declining years.   Though vowed to increased
piety, and more severe penance, her love of literature never deserted her, as was shewn in her
continued efforts towards advancing the art of
printing, and also in her encouragement of all religious works that issued from the press.   In the
year 1504, she caused to be published her translation of " Gerson's imitation of, and following
of Christ."   " The Mirror of Gold" was probably printed about the same time, as the preface
proves it to have been in circulation during the
life of her son, though the actual date of its appearance is not specified in the work itself. It was
printed by Richard Pynson, on fine vellum, beautifully ornamented ; though another edition, by
Wynken de Worde, was printed after the decease
of his liberal patroness.[2]   Very few copies are
now extant of this curious work.

The Countess of Richmond became a third
time a widow, towards the close of 1504, by the

[1] See Appendix H.   [2] Herbert's Typographical Antiquities.

demise of her noble husband, the Earl of Derby,
Lord Stanley, Lord of the Isle of Man, and High
Constable of England, who, after an active and
distinguished career, departed this life at Derby
House, (19th Henry the Seventh). This eminent
nobleman bequeathed to his son-in-law the King,
a cup of gold, and willed that his lady, then
living, should peaceably enjoy all the lordships,
manors, &c. assigned for her jointure. He prays
his majesty to be a good lord to his sons, as he
had been a true servant to him, and charges them,
on his blessing, to do the King good service
during their whole lives.[1]

Henry appears, indeed, to have thoroughly appreciated the noble qualities of his father-in-law,
who continued equally to enjoy his confidence, and
to be as closely in attendance at court as before his
separation from the Lady Margaret, and her voluntary retirement from its cares : to her the attachment of the noble Earl was strikingly evinced,
by his having provided a tomb in the church of the
priory of Bourscough, near Lathom, the burial
place of his ancestors, with effigies of himself and
both his wives, where they were ordered to be
prayed for, and had in perpetual remembrance,
and where, in accordance with his last testament,
dated July, in 1504, he was himself interred.[2]

This period was an eventful one both to the

[1] Collins' Peer. vol. ii. p. 66.   [2] Dugdale's Baron. vol. iii. p. 249.

Countess of Richmond and her son; for it numbered the deaths of many zealous and firm friends. Few perhaps had aided their fortunes more boldly than Sir Reginald Bray, whose faithful services, after frequent rewards, was finally crowned by the brightest honor of British chivalry, the Order of the Garter. The same year recorded his name, with that of the Lord Derby's, among its illustrious dead. [1]

The Lady Margaret, too, was now soon to be deprived of the solace of her esteemed confessor. Dr. Fisher was nominated to the see of Rochester by Henry the Seventh, an unsolicited and voluntary boon, though at the time attributed very naturally to the influence of the Countess of Richmond over her son. The letter from the King to his mother being extant [2] is here introduced as an additional evidence of the strong attachment that existed between them, and also as exhibiting the delicacy that prompted him to ask his parent's acquiescence in a preferment that might have been made to appear as the simple reward of merit, instead, of resulting, as the letter implies, from the additional claims which the singular virtue, holiness, and piety, of the almoner and confessor of Margaret of Richmond, had upon his discerning and approving sovereign.

[1] Testamenta Vetusa, p. 446.
[2] Ex. Regist. Coll. Jo.   (Published by Baker 1708.)

" MADAM,

" An [if] I thought I should not offend you, which
I will never do wilfully, I am well minded to promote Master Fisher your confessor, to a Bishop-
ric ; and I assure you, Madam, for none other
cause, but for the great and singular virtue, that I
know and see in him, as well in cunning and
natural wisdom, and specially for his good and
virtuous living and conversation. And by the
promotion of such a man, I know well it should
corage [encourage] many others to live vertuously
and to take such wages as he doth, which should
be a good example to many others hereafter.
Howbeit without your pleasure known, I will not
move him, nor tempt him therein. And therefore
I beseech you, that I may know your mind and
pleasure in that behalf, which shall be followed as
much as God will give me grace. I have, in my
days, promoted many a man unadvisedly, and I
would now make some recompence to promote
some good and virtuous man which I doubt not,
should best please God, who ever preserve you in
good health and long life."

" King Henry,

" To my Lady Grace his Moder."

Dr. Fisher had previously taken his doctor's
degree, and soon after his elevation to the prelacy

he was elected, in compliment to his benefactress, perpetual Chancellor of the University of Cambridge,[1] being the first instance of such a choice. The austere life and studious habits of this divine, had been the means of attracting the learned Erasmus to the same university.[2] And it was also owing to the persuasion and advice of Bishop Fisher, that the Lady Margaret undertook that great work which sheds such glory on her memory, the foundation of Christ's College, Cambridge. It was built on the site of an Hostel, called God's house, begun by her kinsman Henry the Sixth, but left incomplete owing to the troubles of his turbulent reign. Its recommencement was graced by the presence of Henry the Seventh, who visited Cambridge[3] in the year 1505 for that purpose, and from whom the Countess of Richmond obtained a licence to change its appellation to that of Christ's College. Taking down the former ruinous buildings, she erected the noble edifice that attested to future generations her zeal for the advancement of piety and learning, endowing it liberally with rich manors and valuable lands for the support of a master, twelve fellows, and forty-seven scholars. Superstitious objections having been made in a subsequent reign to this number of fellows, as bearing a reference to our blessed

[1] Baker's Preface, p. x.   [2] Jortin's Life of Erasmus.
[3] Fuller's Ch. Hist. Appendix. p. 89.

Saviour and his twelve disciples, King Edward the
Sixth added a thirteenth fellowship and the number has since been augmented to fifteen. [1]

The attachment borne by the Lady Margaret to
the title she received from her first marriage, and
the associations connected with her brief union
with the young Earl of Richmond, is rendered apparent by two circumstances connected with this
institution which are too interesting to be passed
over unnoticed. The foundation was to be exclusively clerical, and the fellows all to be admitted to priests' orders, as soon as their age
would allow. Six were to be chosen North and
six South of the Trent, but a special exception
was made in favour of candidates natives of Richmondshire, "from which county we take our title." [2]
"Great and good," says Dr. Fuller, "were the lands
which this lady bestowed on this college in several
counties; manors, rents, &c. &c., and Manibere, an
impropriation in Wales; for being of Welsh affinity,
a Tudor by marriage, and having long lived in
Wales where her son King Henry the Seventh was
born; she thought fitting in commemoration thereof to leave some Welsh lands to this her foundation." The building of Christ's College was completed in 1506, and the Bishop of Rochester
appointed visitor for life by the statutes in case

[1] Fuller, p. 91.
[2] "De quo comitatu nos nuncupamur." Ord. Stat.

of the demise of the foundress. She lived however to witness the completion of her noble design,
and was enabled personally to superintend its
progress, as appears from a little incident which
has been recorded shewing the kindliness of her
disposition. Being one day engaged in giving
directions relative to the college, a student who
had fallen into disgrace was forcibly taken by the
superior authorities past her window to receive
correction. " Lente, lente!" she exclaimed, [1] an
expostulation more suited to academic ears, than
an intercession in English, and which, there is
little doubt, secured a pardon to the young
scholar. Her likeness has been preserved in the
chapel of this college by an ancient painting on
wood, as have been also the portraits of her son,
and other of her kindred, on glass in the east
window of the same building.

This great work was scarcely completed, before
the Lady Margaret commenced her last and most
magnificent undertaking, that of St. John's College, for the founding of which she obtained the
king's licence early in 1508. Having munifi-
cently patronised the University of Cambridge,
by her divinity professorship, together with the
perpetual preachership, as also by the endowment of Christ's College, she had contemplated
in accordance with the usage of the time, to devote

[1] Fuller's Church History, Appendix, p. 89.

the remainder of her abundant riches to charitable
donations, or testamentary bequests to Westminster Abbey, the destined place of her burial;
to which holy pile she had in consequence of that
intent been a considerable benefactress, having endowed it with revenues to the value of eighty-seven
pounds per annum.[1] In the Lansdowne MSS.
have been preserved indentures made by her at this
time with the Abbot of Westminster, to pray for
the souls of herself and all her relatives.* Her
son, grandchildren, and husbands are separately
named, and this document is deserving of notice,
because it has always been considered remarkable, that in a similar instrument relating to her
collegiate foundation of Cambridge, no notice
whatever is taken either of her second or third
husband; and the armorial bearings of Sir Henry
Stafford, whose Will shews the strongest affection for the Lady Margaret, are wholly omitted
amongst the elaborate heraldic embellishments

[1] Baker's Preface, p. viii.

* The Abbot and Monastery to pray for the souls of the
Princess Margaret, the King her son, and his children;
Edmund, Earl of Richmond; John, Duke of Somerset and
his wife, the father and mother of the Princess Margaret and
of all her progenitors; Thomas, Earl of Derby, and Henry
Lord Stafford, her late husbands; Elizabeth late Queen of
England and her children, and for all the souls that the said
Princess Margaret shall have prayed for. (Lansdowne MSS.
441. Indentures with the Abbot of Westminster.)

Q

which ornament her magnificent tomb in Westminster Abbey. [1]

To return however to the subject of her collegiate
institutions. She was induced by the influence of
the Bishop of Rochester, [2] to bestow attention on
a monastic establishment in the diocese of her
son-in-law, James Stanley, Bishop of Ely, which
had fallen into great discredit from the irregularity
and misconduct of its members; and after satisfying herself of the validity of the arguments of her
zealous adviser, she was led to change her design
as regarded Westminster, and instead of the ceremonies for the " repose of the soul " after death,
enjoined by the Romish clergy, she nobly resolved
on appropriating the bulk of her wealth towards
erecting and endowing another college for the
advancement of true religion and useful learning.

How refreshing is it to dwell on the enlarged
views which influenced the decision of those who,
like the great and gifted Margaret, born in a
distant age, seemed destined to kindle the torch
of knowledge and hand it on to their successors;
especially when, as in her case, the prejudices
of education, and the weaknesses of declining
years yielded to enlarged views and energy of
intellect. . Her resolution once formed, the Lady
Margaret took speedy measures for the dissolu-

[1] Masters's Life of Thomas Baker, p. 149.
[2] Baker's Preface to Funeral Sermon, p. 13.

tion of the obnoxious monastery, which had
originally been an ancient hospital for canons
regular, built by Nigel, Bishop of Ely, in
1134; but subsequently converted by one of his
successors, into a priory dedicated to St. John the
Evangelist, from whence was derived the appellation of the present collegiate establishment, which
she erected on the site of the old building; richly
endowing it for the support of a master, fifty
fellows, and a proportionate number of scholars.

Before, however, the necessary instrument could
pass through all the legal forms, a heavy affliction
awaited the munificent foundress. She was called
upon to evince her resignation to the will of
Heaven, by submitting with fortitude to the
greatest trial she had yet experienced, by the death
of her son, King Henry the Seventh, who expired
at his palace of Richmond, on the 22nd of April
1508, in the fifty-second year of his age, and the
twenty-fourth of his reign.[1] He had for some
time been suffering from the gout, and his constitution was prematurely enfeebled by the harass-
ing life, and severe privations which had marked
the prime of his days; but that no immediate idea
of his dissolution was entertained, is apparent from
the treaty of marriage which had recently been
contemplated between himself and the Duchess
Dowager of Savoy. The grief of his venerable

[1] Bacon's Hen. VII. pp. 229, and 232.

parent was such as might be imagined from the
strong affection which had ever subsisted between
the mother and son ; and her vigorous health until
then unbroken, except by the severity of her religious mortifications, now became irrecoverably injured by the intensity of her sorrow, and her unceasing struggles to subdue the feelings of nature,
which she believed to be opposed to her earnest desire of submitting in all things to the will of her God.
The deceased Monarch, who had throughout his
troubled reign, manifested the highest respect for
the opinions of the Lady Margaret, and is known
to have been greatly influenced by her in the
tuition of his children, and the regulation of his
domestic affairs, evinced to the last his sense of
her energetic character by leaving her the executrix of his Will,[1] styling her " our dearest and
most entirely beloved Mother, Margaret Countess
of Richmond."

Her first act justified the high trust reposed
in her, and was fully in accordance with that
vigour of mind, which never wasted its strength
in unavailing sorrow, or weakened its useful
powers by selfish and desponding grief.   She
drew up a list of such personages as were most
esteemed and trusted by the late King, out of
whom she selected a few of the most exemplary
and intelligent, as councillors to her grandson

[1] Testamenta Vetusta, p. 26.

the youthful monarch, and to influence with their wisdom, and controul by their integrity the opening acts of his reign.[1]

The funeral of King Henry the Seventh, was one of the most pompous and magnificent in the annals of England, and befitting in all respects the sumptuous chapel which that King had prepared in Westminster Abbey for the interment of himself and his family. His successor retired from Richmond on the decease of his royal parent, and as a mark of respect to his memory, dwelt privately in the Tower of London[2] until after the funeral obsequies were performed; when by reason of his double claim to the crown, in right of his father, and of his mother as the heiress of the house of York, he was proclaimed King by the title of Henry the Eighth. He ascended the throne with brighter promises of excellence than can usually be anticipated at the age of eighteen, principally from the attention which had early been bestowed on his education by the Countess of Richmond. The funeral sermon for the deceased sovereign was preached by the Bishop of Rochester, and the closing acts of his reign were marked by deeds worthy the offspring of so pious a parent. He discharged all persons who were imprisoned for debt under forty shillings, com-

[1] Herbert's Hen. VIII. p. 2 and 4.
[2] Ibid. p. 1.

pleted numerous religious foundations, and gave
an increase to his public and private alms; grant-
ing a general pardon throughout his realm, and
ordaining by his Will, that restitution should
be made to his subjects of all sums which had
been unjustly taken by subordinate officers.[1]   With
such evident proofs of piety and christian feeling the son of " the admirable Margaret" sank
to rest.

Few monarchs have had greater injustice done
to their memory,—arising from the little allowance made for the difficult period in which he
was called to the throne—than Henry the Seventh.
His early trials and misfortunes, had enabled
him to perceive that the ambition and absolute
power of the clergy and nobles, united to the
servile and debasing vassalage of the popu-
lace of England, had been the chief cause of the
misery that for so many ages had impoverished
and degraded the land.   He struck at the root of
this evil.   Adversity had been his school, and
prosperity brought to remembrance the sorrowful
days of youth, and the ineffectual struggles of
manhood.   By endeavouring to deprive the clergy
of their abused and miscalled religious sanctuaries,[2]
and by diminishing with a strong arm the feudal
authority and despotic power of the nobles; by

[1] Bacon's Hen. VII. pp. 229 and 231.
[2] See Appendix I.

seeking to create a more independent spirit in the oppressed people, and to lighten the bondage of the enslaved vassals, King Henry made the two great powers of his realm his avowed enemies, and did not live long enough to reap benefit from those other classes of the community for whom he ultimately procured that independent and glorious liberty, which succeeding generations could alone appreciate, and which the present age enjoy both in church and state. This wise and politic Monarch, moreover, promoted the social arts, and subdued the warlike ferocity of the times by patronizing trade and commerce. He aided his illustrious mother, in fostering by his encouragement, the growth of literature, and thereby most effectually advanced the cause of piety and religion; and while his subjects, in the romance of by-gone days, anticipated in him, an Arthur, they found that their ruler indeed proved himself to them,—as he has done to succeeding generations,—a second Alfred.

With the venerable Margaret the charm of life was gone when she resigned into the hands of her Maker, her loved and only son. She had survived parents, husbands, offspring, and kindred: her whole thoughts were now on heaven; and she was solely occupied in making her peace with God, and preparing to join in a better state of existence, those so tenderly loved on earth. Her pious biographer, in narrating the close of her career, says "that her eyes were spent with weeping and tears, sometimes of devotion, sometimes of penitence; her ears in hearing the word of God and the divine service which daily was kept in her chapel; that her tongue was occupied in prayer much part of the day, her legs and feet in visiting the altars, and other holy places; her hands in giving alms to the poor and needy, dressing them when they were sick, and ministering unto them meat and drink."[1]   Her public acts were in accordance with these her private and daily preparations for another world.   She founded an alms-house near Westminster Abbey for indigent women,[2] endowed a similar institution at Hatfield for twelve infirm deserving persons;[3] and maintained divers poor scholars at Oxford, providing them with a tutor at her sole expense.[4]

In addition to the devotional works already mentioned, she farther commanded, at this mournful period, the printing of the seven penitential psalms, compiled by Fisher, Bishop of Rochester.   Likewise, the " Stultifera Navis,"[5] or " Ship of Fooles of this World," rendered into prose at her express

[1] Fisher's Funeral Sermon, p. 20.
[2] Stowe's Survey of London, p. 525.
[3] See Countess of Richmond's Will.
[4] Mag. Brit. Oxfordshire, p. 277.
[5] Walpole's Royal Authors.

command, by Henry Watson, and published by her printer, Wynken de Worde, in 1509.*

The only remaining temporal anxiety of the declining Countess were the legal forms requisite for completing the endowment of St. John's College, which had been delayed by the decease of her royal son. She had amply provided against all evil that might possibly ensue from her approaching death, by means of a codicil to her Will, clearly and carefully securing to this noble institution lands in the counties of Devon, Somerset, and Northampton, amounting to four hundred pounds a-year, exclusive of the revenues of the old priory, with which it was incorporated, and a mortmain of fifty pounds per annum ;[1] a most munificent provision at a time, when " twelve pence per week was allowed in commons to a Fellow, and only seven pence a week to a Scholar."[2] Nevertheless, she earnestly desired to witness the fulfilment of her designs, that she might feel secure against those mischances which often frustrate the views of the best intentioned. But, alas!

* This very curious work was written by Alexander Barclay, to expose and reprobate the indecorous behaviour which was at that time common in churches, where, in defiance of all reverence and religious feeling, individuals would bring into the temple of God their hawks and hounds, disturbing the devotion of those who came to pray, by noisy and clamorous meetings, and absolute disregard of the sacred precincts.

[1] Nichol's Royal Wills, p. 395.   [2] Baker's Preface, p. xlv.

the web of life had been spun to its utmost.   The
threads which had snapped asunder, when Henry
the Seventh expired, could never be re-united.

The learned establishment, whose foundation
she had so much at heart, was begun, planned,
and richly endowed, by its munificent foundress;
but the completion of the work remained for those
chosen executors to whom she assigned the great
trust, in the full confidence that they would not
suffer her pious intentions to remain unfulfilled.
She felt her end approaching, but it was by increasing bodily infirmities, not by decay of her
mental powers, which, to the last, remained un-
impaired, but through the testimony of her faithful spiritual attendant,[1] we learn that her sufferings
were so acute, that her piteous cries would arouse
tears in those devoted friends whom her goodness
had assembled around her, to minister to her
wants, and soften, by their gentle attentions, the
rugged path that led to the tomb.

Full of faith in her Redeemer, and trust in her
God, bemoaning the infirmity of her own nature,
but dispensing charity to others, even in her dying
hour, the Countess of Richmond expired at Westminster on the 29th of June, 1509,[2] three months
only after her son's decease, and in the sixty-ninth
year of her age, retaining, to the last moment of

[1] Fisher's Funeral Sermon, p. 21.
[2] Sandford s Geneal. Hist. p. 328.

her existence, those high resources and vigorous powers, that calm resignation and unsubdued
fortitude, which can only result from a religious
and well disciplined mind ; from a conscience de-
void of reproach, arising from a well spent and devotional life.   She was interred in King Henry
the Seventh's chapel, where a superb altar tomb
of black marble, enclosed by a grate, and surmounted with her statue, is erected to her memory.

But Margaret of Lancaster needed no superb
tomb, no splendid statue, no pompous record, to fix
her remembrance in the minds either of that age, or
of those which were to come.   She was enshrined in
the heart of all good men, of the disinterested pa-
triot, the religious churchman, the humble student.
But most of all, she lived in the hearts of the suffering poor.   Yet how could a life of such active
benevolence fail of securing to her, at the approach
of death, the sympathy and support of friends,
whose deep and fervent love survived the revered
object who had won their admiration, their respect,
and their attachment. Erasmus, the great and learned, who has recorded her virtues and good deeds,
wrote the simple epitaph,[1] reciting her charities,
which is inscribed round the verge of her tomb.[2]

[1] See Appendix, K.

[2] " For the drawing up of which," says Baker, in his pre-
face, p. xix. " he had a reward of twenty shillings from the
University of Cambridge, as is entered in a Computus, or old
Book of Accounts."

The Bishop of Rochester, who, as her confessor and spiritual guide, had long been in possession of her most secret thoughts, preached her funeral sermon, and has therein recorded the chief particulars of her private career and domestic virtues. Partial, no doubt, he might have been, for she was his benefactress and personal friend; but the deeds he describes are corroborated by existing testimonials, which have proved to posterity that her works in public were dedicated to God's glory, rather than to her own, whilst her private charities could not only be best proclaimed by, but in reality could only be known to him, who, as her almoner, and the dispenser of ner secret bounty, was the best witness of the genuine and active benevolence of her heart. She was the friend of the friendless, the comforter of the afflicted, the munificent patroness of learning, the meek, but strenuous supporter of religion. Such were the noble characteristics of the dignified Countess of Richmond and Derby.

As her actions seem, by their enlightened tendency, to have been in advance of the age in which she was born, so did the fame of her virtues outlive the period in which she died. The impression which her singular goodness and early precepts had made on the mind of her grandson, Henry the Eighth, induced him, in after life, when pillaging other religious houses, to spare the cathedral of St. David's, where the husband of her youth was interred ; to abstain from demolishing the chauntry she had founded at Wimborne minster, to perpetuate the memory of her parents ; and to sanction the completion of St. John's College, Cambridge, though he abstracted as much from the wealth with which she had endowed it as his rapacity could legally claim in right of inheritance.

One of the last acts of his aged grandmother was to commend the youthful monarch's inexperience to the excellent Bishop Fisher. What a pang was she spared, when, after having witnessed the promise of good which he early displayed under her immediate nurture, this King became, in succeeding years, the inhuman murderer of the eminent divine, under whose tutelage he imbibed that knowledge which rendered the opening of his reign so auspicious.

To the latest moment of her eventful life the Countess of Richmond gave proof of her strong judgment and foresight, in leaving the learned prelate one of her executors, and the chief agent in prosecuting her collegiate endowments ; as his zeal and perseverance alone overcame the difficulties which were placed in the way of the further progress of the building, and which increased tenfold after the death of the Lady Margaret. Worn out by continued oppositions, the undaunted prelate

at last appealed to the see of Rome,[1] and the Bull
granted by Pope Julius the Second was too decisive
to be resisted even by the King himself. The
charter of the foundation is dated April 9th, 1511,
when the building was commenced. It was
completed at the then enormous expense of
5000l., and at length was opened in great form
by its zealous and indefatigable superior in 1516,
for a master and thirty-one fellows, but by the
liberality of succeeding benefactors they have
since been augmented. This college whose foundation was the last and the most important of
the Countess of Richmond's great deeds, contains
three extremely curious portraits of the foundress ;
in all of which she is represented in an attitude of
devotion, and in the habit of a recluse or nun.
Over the entrance, in the first court in a niche, is
placed her statue, and few pass on to the hall without stopping to gaze on the worn and attenuated
figure of the " Venerable Margaret."[*]

By her Will she bequeathed ample means for
confirming and continuing her many charities ;
and four days before her decease, she evinced
that confidence in others, and displayed that
mistrust of herself which formed so beautiful

[1] Baker's Preface, p. 22.

[*] Through the courtesy of the late Master and Fellows of
St. John's, a copy of the fine original painting, which adorns
the Hall of their college, has been permitted to be engraved for
the frontispiece of this Memoir.

a feature in her character, by submitting her last
testament to the supervision of her Chancellor,
Dr. Henry Hornby, in conjunction with Bishop
Fox ; that they might alter, add, or diminish as in
their sadness they thought convenient."[1]

She left a fine library of books in English,
French, and Latin, and on a small tablet near her
monument in Westminster Abbey, is a Latin
elegy written by John Skelton, the poet laureate, dated 16th August, 1516. Her magnificent tomb was the production of the skilful
Florentine sculptor, " Pietro Torregiano," the
contemporary of Michael Angelo. The " Mornynge remembrance" or funeral sermon, preached
by Bishop Fisher, was printed by Wynken de
Worde shortly after her decease, and was re-
published, with a valuable preface, by the Rev.
Thomas Baker, the celebrated antiquary and fellow of her college of St. John's, in 1708.

Her order of precedence is preserved in the
Harleian MSS.; and her Will, which is extremely
curious, is deposited in the Prerogative court of
Canterbury.* Her public institutions attest the
munificence with which she sought to further the
advancement of literature, and her wealthy en-

[1] Baker's Preface, p. 50.

* The most important and most striking portions of the
Lady Margaret's Will, are contained in an abstract annexed
to this Memoir.

dowments have enabled hundreds of students to drink deeply at the fountain of knowledge.

But, to dwell longer on the merits and rare excellence of her character is needless. She has been commemorated by Shakspeare, and her memory has been immortalized by the poet Gray. To such praise it might well have sufficed to have left the subject of this memoir, but, as before said, a more expressive, a more enduring monument than even the poet's eulogy is the simple mention of a great name; and that eulogy is in a high degree conveyed in the all-sufficient designation of " the Lady Margaret." No expletive is requisite, no further definition required to denote her who was the earliest of English female authors, and one of the most distinguished of England's noble women; whose whole life affords a bright example of goodness, religion, and morality, and by whose virtuous career the female sex has been alike elevated, dignified, and adorned.

Such was the parent of King Henry the Seventh, such the ancestress of our present youthful sovereign; the progenitrix of a long and glorious race,—the benefactress of generations yet unborn; the noble-minded, but unassuming— the pious—the admirable—the illustrious

MARGARET BEAUFORT.

THE WILL OF MARGARET BEAUFORT.

The Countess of Richmond's Will is so remarkable a document, and so illustrative of her character, that her life can scarcely be considered to
have been faithfully recorded, without the inser-
tion of this, her last act. Its great length, however,
arising from her innumerable charities, and the
minute detail of religious observances, connected
with the Romish Church, precludes the possibility
of the deed being inserted entire in this Memoir.
Nevertheless, considering that so valuable a record of the Lady Margaret's justice and munificence ought not to be wholly passed over without
notice, her voluminous Testament and Codicil
have been attentively examined, and such portions
carefully selected, as were considered character-
istic of her private and domestic feelings, or interesting from their connexion with her public acts.
The whole document has been printed literally, in
" Nichols' Collection of Royal Wills," with the
addition of Explanatory Notes, and a copious
Glossary.

" In the Name of ALMIGHTY GOD, Amen.

" We, Margaret Countess of Richmond and Derby, mother to the most excellent Prince King Henry the Seventh, by the grace of GOD, King of England and of France, and Lord of Ireland, our most dear son, have called to our remembrance the unstableness of this transitory world, and that every creature here living is mortal, and the time and place of death to every creature uncertain. And also calling to our remembrance the great rewards of eternal life, that every Christian creature, in stedfast faith of holy church, shall have for their good deeds done by them in their present life. We, therefore, being of whole and good mind, &c. the vi day of June, the year of our Lord God a thousand five hundred and eight, and in the xxiii year of the reign of our said most dear son the King, make, ordain, and declare, our testament and last will, in manner and form following : that is to say, First, we give and bequeath our soul to Almighty God, to our blessed Lady, Saint Mary the Virgin, and to all the holy company in heaven. And our body to be buried in the monastery of Saint Peter of Westminster, in such convenable place as we in our life, or our executors after our decease, shall provide for the same within the Chapel of our Lady, which is now begun by the said our most dear son. Item, we will that placebo and dirige with lauds, and with all divine services, prayers, and observance be-

longing thereunto, be solemnly and devoutly sung and
said in the day of our decease, by all the priests, ministers, and children of our chapel.........in as solemn and
devout wise, as they can do or devise, and so to continue to sing and say daily, every day from to day, as long
as our body shall rest there unremoved toward the said
place of interment.   Item we will, that our executors,
as soon as they conveniently may, after our decease,
cause solemnly and devoutly to be sung or said for our
soul in every xv parish churches next adjoining to the
place of our decease, by all the priests, clerks, and ministers of every such church, placebo, dirige, &c. &c.

   ... ...

"Item, we will, that in the day that it shall please Almighty God to call us from this present and transitory
life to his infinite mercy and grace, and in the day of our
interment, there to be distributed in alms amongst poor
people, by the discretion of our executors cxxxiii li.
vis. viiid. or more, as it shall be thought convenient by
their discretions.   And cc li. to be disposed in buying
of cloth for our executors and servants, men and women,
or other persons, that shall give their attendance upon
the conveyance of our body and our said interment, and
at our month's day.

"Item,—We will that our executors, in as goodly
haste and brief time as they can or may, after our decease, content and pay all our debts.   And we will that
our said executors cause all our household servants to
be kept together, and household kept in all things convenient for them at and in such convenient place as
shall be thought by our executors most necessary for
the same, from the time of our decease by the space of
one quarter of a year at the least.   And that our exe-

cutors, by all the same time, shall provide and ordain, or cause to be provided and ordained for all our said household servants; that is to say, for as many of them as will there so tarry and abide by all the said time, meat, drink, and other things convenient for household, as they have used and accustomed to have had heretofore in our household. And also to content and pay to every of our household servants, both man and woman, their wages for one-half year next after our decease, as well to them that will depart within the quarter of one year after our decease, as to them that will tarry and abide together in household during all the same quarter .... And of this present our testament and last will, we make and ordain our executors, Richard, Bishop of Winchester; John, Bishop of Rochester; my Lord Herbert, the King's Chamberlain; Sir Thomas Lovell, Treasurer of the King's Household; Sir Henry Marney, Chancellor of the Duchy of Lancaster; Sir John St. John, our Chamberlain; Henry Hornby, our Chancellor; Sir Hugh Ashton, Comptroller of our household. And we, in our most humble wise, heartily pray and beseech the King, our sovereign Lord and most dear son, that it would please his Highness to be supervisor of this our present testament and last will, and to be good and gracious Lord, and to shew his special favour, help, and assistance to our said executors, and to every of them, in executing and performing, of this our present testament and last will. And also, that it would please his Highness to see and cause as well all the premises afore rehearsed, as all that hereafter is specified in this our present testament and last will, or in the said schedule thereunto annexed, or that shall be contained in any other writing or codicil to be hereafter hereunto annexed to be well and truly executed and performed in every behalf, for the singular love that we bare, and ever have borne unto his Highness, as he will have our blessing, and be discharged before God, and for the singular trust we have in the same.

" And forasmuch as the singular laud, praise and pleasure of ALMIGHTY GOD resteth much in this transitory world in administration of sacrifices and divine services, by the ministers of holy church, for remission of our sins, and in the increase of virtue—cunning [*knowledge*], and of all Christian faith.................therefore we, intending, with the grace of ALMIGHTY GOD, to cause him to be the more honoured and served, as well within the said monastery, where we intend, with God's grace, our body to be interred, as in the Universities of Oxford and Cambridge, and other places where the laws of God be more specially learned, taught and preached; and scholars to the same intent, to be brought up in virtue and cunning: for the increase of Christ's faith, have provided, ordained, and established, as followeth: three perpetual daily masses, with divine services and observance, and one perpetual anniversary to be yearly, solemnly, and devoutly holden and kept......and with the distribution of x li. in alms at every such anniversary, for the health of our soul perpetually, while the world shall endure, &c. And also have provided, established, and founden by the King's licence, two perpetual readers in holy theology, one of them in the University of Cambridge, and another of them in the University of Oxford, and one perpetual preacher of the word of God in the said University of Cambridge. And have licence to found a perpetual chauntry in the church of Wimborne, of one perpetual priest to teach grammar freely to all them that will come thereunto

perpetually while the world shall endure :.................
And also, whereas King Henry VIth of blessed memory, was in mind and purpose to have provided and
ordained in a place in Cambridge, called then God's
house, scholars to the number of LX, there to learn and
study in all liberal science, in which place was never
scholars fellows of the same place above the number of
four for lack of exhibition and finding, we have now of
late purchased and obtained licence of the said King,
our most dear son, and by reason thereof have founded
and established in the same place a college, called
Christ's College, of a master, xii scholars fellows, and
XLVII scholars disciples, there to be perpetually
founden, and brought up in learning, virtue and cunning, according to such statutes and ordinances as we
have made, and shall make for the same.................
For the exhibition and perpetual finding of the said two
perpetual readers in the said Universities of Oxford and
Cambridge, to either of the same two readers an annuity of xiii li. vi s. viiid. yearly. And also......... to
the said perpetual preacher an annuity of x li. for his
exhibition and perpetual finding in such manner and
form as in the deeds more plainly appeareth.

" Item—We will that our executors, as soon as they
conveniently may after our decease, do make, or cause
to be made in the chapel there, as our body shall be interred, a convenient tomb by their discretions; and
one altar, or two, in the same chapel for the said two
chauntry masses there perpetually to be said at the hours
and times, and with all such prayers and observances as
is before rehearsed................And we, in our most
humble wise, also pray the King, our most dear son, to
give his gracious assent thereto, to suffer, and assist our

executors and assignees so to do, as we put our singular
trust in his Highness. And we the said Princess, after
our debts paid, and after our legacies and bequests specified in this our present testament and last will, and in
the schedules thereunto annexed, fully and truly in
every thing executed and performed, will, that our executors, calling into their inward minds and remembrance Almighty God, and the duties of executors for
distribution of goods, to them, in such case committed,
to distribute the residue of all our said goods for the
wealthe of our soul, in such wise as by their discretion
shall be thought most best, meritorious, and convenient.
In witness whereof, to these presents we have set to
our sign manual and seal of arms, the day and year
abovesaid.

Ultima Voluntas ejusdem D'ne Margarete.

Be it remembered.—That it was also the last will of
the said Princess to dissolve the hospital of Saint John
in Cambridge, and to alter and to found thereof a college of secular persons; that is to say, a master and fifty
scholars, with divers servants; and new to build the
said college, and sufficiently to endow the same with
lands and tenements, after the manner and form of other
colleges in Cambridge: and to furnish the same, as
well in the chapel library, pantry, and kitchen, with
books and all other things necessary for the same.

Also, the said Princess willed, that her household
servants, which had long continued and done to her
good service, should be rewarded with part of her goods,
by the discretion of the Rev. Father in God, Richard
Bishop of Winchester, upon information given unto
him of their good service and merits; and in likewise

she would, that by his discretion her executors should be
rewarded. Also, the said Princess willed that the number of xii poor men and women, that her grace kept and
founded at Hatfield in her lifetime, should be kept and
maintained at her costs during all the lives of the said
poor men and women..........................Also, the said
Princess willed that Christ's College should, at her costs
and charge, be perfectly finished in all reparations,
building and garnishing of the same. Also, the said
Princess willed that said manor of Malton, in the shire
of Cambridge, which belongeth to the said Christ's College, should be sufficiently builded and repaired at her
cost and charge; so that the said masters and scholars
may resort thither, and there to tarry in time of conta-
gious sickness at Cambridge, and exercise their learning and studies. Also, the said Princess willed that a
strong coffer should be provided in the said Christ's
College, at her costs and charge; also, that her executors should put in the same c li. of money, or more, for
the use of the said College, to be spended as they shall
need. Also, the said Princess willed, that all her plate,
jewels, vestments, altar-clothes, books, hangings, and
other necessaries belonging to her chapel in the time of
her decease, and not otherwise bequeathed, should be
divided between her said Colleges of Christ and St.
John, by the discretion of her executors. Also, the said
Princess willed, the fourth day before her decease, that
the Rev. Father in God, Richard, Bishop of Winchester, and Master Henry Hornby, her Chancellor, should
the same day have the oversight of her said will and testament, and by their sadness and good discretion, should
have full authority and power to alter, add to, and dimi-

nish, such articles in our said will and testament as they thought most convenient, and according to the will of the said Princess.

Probat' dict' testamenti apud Lambith, xvii die mensis Octobris, Anno Domini Mill'imo Quingentessimo xii°

A TABLE SHEWING THE DESCENT OF THE COUNTESS OF RICHMOND.

KING EDWARD III. ob. 1377.

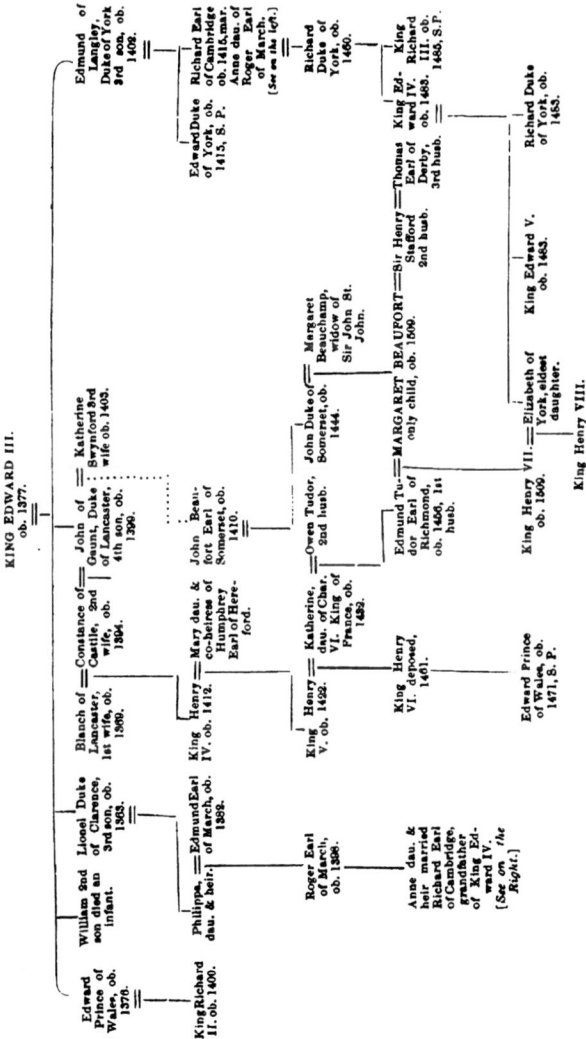

Edward Prince of Wales, ob. 1376.

William 2nd son died an infant.

Lionel Duke of Clarence, 3rd son, ob. 1363.

Blanch of Lancaster, 1st wife, ob. 1369. == John of Gaunt, Duke of Lancaster, 4th son, ob. 1399. == Constance of Castile, 2nd wife, ob. 1394. == Katherine Swynford 3rd wife ob. 1403.

Edmund of Langley, Duke of York, 3rd son, ob. 1402.

KingRichard II. ob. 1400.

Phillippa, dau. & heir. == EdmundEarl of March, ob. 1389.

King Henry IV. ob. 1412. == Mary dau. & co-heiress of Humphrey Earl of Hereford.

John Beaufort Earl of Somerset, ob. 1410.

Edward Duke of York, ob. 1415, S. P.

Richard Earl of Cambridge ob. 1415, mar. Anne dau. of Roger Earl of March. [See on the left.]

Roger Earl of March, ob. 1398.

King Henry V. ob. 1422. == Katherine, dau. of Chas. VI. King of France, ob. 1482.

John Duke of Somerset, ob. 1444. == Margaret Beauchamp, widow of Sir John St. John.

Richard Duke of York, ob. 1460.

Anne dau. & heir married Richard Earl of Cambridge, grandfather of King Edward IV. [See on the Right.]

King Henry VI. deposed, 1461.

Owen Tudor, 2nd husb.

MARGARET BEAUFORT only child, ob. 1509. == Sir Henry Stafford, 2nd husb. == Thomas Earl of Derby, 3rd husb.

King Edward IV. ob. 1483.

King Richard III. ob. 1485, S.P.

Edward Prince of Wales, ob. 1471, S. P.

Edmund Tudor Earl of Richmond, ob. 1456, 1st husb.

King Henry VII. ob. 1509. == Elizabeth of York, eldest daughter.

King Edward V. ob. 1483.

Richard Duke of York, ob. 1483.

King Henry VIII.

APPENDIX.

A.

GRANT TO THE DUKE OF SUFFOLK OF THE WARDSHIP OF
MARGARET BEAUFORT, 22 HEN. VI., 1444.

(See p. 23.)

" By the King.

" Right reverend Father in God, right trusty and right well-
beloved, we greet you well.   And forasmuch as our cousin
the Duke of Somerset is now late passed to God's mercy, the
which hath a daughter and heir to succeed after him of full
tender age, called Margaret; we consider the notable services
that our cousin the Earl of Suffolk hath done unto us, and
tendering him therefore the more specially, as reason will,
have of our grace and especial proper motion and mere delibe-
ration granted unto him to have the ward and marriage of the
said Margaret, without any thing therefore unto us or our heirs
yielding : wherefore we will and charge you that unto our said
cousin of Suffolk ye do make upon this our grant, our letters
patents sufficient in law, and in due form; and that ye fail
not hereof, as we especially trust you, and as ye desire to do
unto us singular pleasure, and that ye send unto us our said
letters patents sealed by the bearer of these.

Letting you wit, that ye shall hereafter, at such time as ye

come unto our presence, have such warrant for your discharge
in this behalf as shall be sufficient unto you, and as the case
requireth.

Given under our signet, at our Castle of Berkhampstead, the
last day of May.

To the right reverend father in God, our right trusty and
right well-beloved the Archbishop of Canterbury, our Chancellor of England.[1]

———

B.

EXTRACT FROM THE PATENT OF LEGITIMATION GRANTED
BY KING RICHARD II., FEB. 1397,[2] SHEWING THE INTERLI-
NEATION, SUPPOSED TO HAVE BEEN INSERTED BY HENRY
IV., IN 1407,[3] WHEN AT THE REQUEST OF THE EARL OF
SOMERSET, HE EXEMPLIFIED AND CONFIRMED THE GRANT.

(See p. 82.)

" We do, in the fullness of our royal power, and by the assent
of parliament, by the tenor of these presents, empower you to
be raised, promoted, elected, assume, and be admitted to all
honours, dignities [*except to the royal dignity*[*]] pre-eminen-
ces, estates, and offices, public and private, whatsoever, as well
perpetual as temporal."

Witnessed by the King at Westminster, the 9th day of February.

[1] See the remarks on this subject in the Excerpta Historica. p. 3.

[2] Rot. Parl. 20 Rich. II.—No. 28, Vol. iii. p. 303.

[3] The patent of legitimation was exemplified and confirmed by King
Henry IV. on the 10th February, 1407.

[*] Interlined in the copy on the patent Rolls, 20 Rich. II., p. 2. m. 6.

C.

EXTRACTS FROM THE WILL OF SIR HARRY STAFFORD, KNIGHT, SON OF THE NOBLE PRINCE HUMPHREY, DUKE OF BUCKINGHAM.

(See p. 105.)

" Item. I bequeath to the high altar of the parish church of Woking, for my tithes and offerings forgotten or withholden, xs.

Item. I bequeath to the works of the said church of Woking, xxs.

Item. I bequeath to my son-in-law, the Earl of Richmond, a trappur, and four new horse harness of blue velvet.

Item. I bequeath to my brother John, Earl of Wiltshire, my bay courser.

Item. I bequeath to Reynold Bray, my Receiver-general, my grizzled horse. And the residue of all my goods, catalogues, and debts, wheresoever they be—after my debts that I owe paid, my funeral expenses done, and this my testament fulfilled,—I give and bequeath to mine entirely beloved wife Margaret, Countess of Richmond, she thereof to dispose her own free will for evermore.

Witnesses, John Geffrey, Walter Baker, vicar of the parish church of Woking, aforesaid.

Sir Richard Brigge, prior of the priory of Newark.

Probatum iiij. May M cccc Lxxxj.

Extracted from the Registry of the Prerogative Court of Canterbury.

D.

KING RICHARD NOT DEFORMED.

(See p. 154.)

" As far without the certainty of a proofe, is the pretended deformity of his body which is controverted by many; some peremptorily asserted he was not deformed, of which opinion was John Stow, a man indifferently inquisitive (as in all their other affairs,) after the verball relations and persons of princes, and curious in his description of their features and lineaments, who in all his inquiry could finde no such note of deformitie in this King; but hath acknowledged vivâ voce that he had spoken with some ancient men, who from their owne sight and knowledge affirmed he was of bodily shape, comely enough, onely of low stature, which is all the deformitie they proportion so monstrously; neither did John Rouce, who knew him, and writ much in his description, observe any other; and Archienbald Qhuitlaw, ambassador unto this King from Scotland, in his oration says, he had *corpus exiguum;* not otherwise; so (to my conceit) Philip de Comines and the Prior de Croyland (who had seen and knowne this prince,) seeme to cleere him implicatively; for in all their discourses of him they never directly nor indirectly, covertly or apertly, insinuate this deformity, which (I suppose,) they would not have passed. And Sir Thomas More himselfe, doth not certainly affirme the deformity, but rather seemes to take it as a malitious report; for, saith he, King Richard was deformed as the fame ranne by those that hated him." Buck's Life of Richard III., p. 79, 80.   See also Polidore Virgil, p. 544.   Walpole's Historic Doubts, p. 102.   Sharon Turner, vol. iii. p. 477, who, after stating that Richard was short, and his figure weakened by illness, adds " for the hump back and crooked form," I think we have no adequate authority.

E.

•

TESTIMONY IN FAVOUR OF THE BELIEF THAT PERKIN WAR-
BECK WAS RICHARD DUKE OF YORK.

(See p. 183.)

" In vulgus fama valuit filios Edwardi Regis aliquò terra-
rum partem migrasse, atque ita superstites esse. Thus, Polidore
Virgil (l. 2. 6.) with which Dr. Morton and Sir Thomas
More agree in one place. The man (say they) commonly
called Perkin Warbeck was, as well with the princes as with
the people, English and foreign, held to be the younger son of
Edward the Fourth, and that the deaths of the young King
Edward, and of Richard his brother had come so far in ques-
tion, as some are yet in doubt whether they were destroyed or
no, in the days of King Richard. By which it appears they
were thought to be living after his death. Another author
and more ancient agreeth with them, ' Vulgatum est Regis
Edwardi pueros concessisse in fata, sed quo genere interitus
ignoratur' (Prior of Croyland). Let us now take a more particular view of those witnesses who stood for Perkin. Sir
Robert Clifford served King Edward very neare, and in good
credit, so could not but have an assured knowledge of the
King's sons, and was therefore the more particularly sent to
certifie his knowledge, who certainely affirmed him to bee the
younger son of Edward IV., and confirmed many with him,
such as had likewise served King Edward, and had been ac-
quainted with the prince his conveying beyond sea, though
much was done to alter Sir Robert's opinion ; the Lord Fitz-
Walter was of the same belief, and avowed Perkin, the true
Duke of York most constantly unto death ; as resolute was
Sir William Stanley, though he were Lord Chamberlain to
Henry VII., and in great favour ; Sir George Neville, Sir
Simon Mountford, Sir William Daubeny, Sir Thomas Thwaits,
Sir Robert Ratcliffe, Sir John Taylor, Sir Thomas Chaloner,
Thomas Bagnall, with many other gentlemen of quality, all

maintained him to be the Duke of York, son of Edward the
Fourth; and sundry of the clergy who had been chaplains to
the king his father, or otherwise occasioned to attend the court,
as Dr. Rochford, Dr. Poynes, Dr. Sutton, Dr. Worsley, Dean
of St. Paul's, Dr. Leyborn, Dr. Lesly, with many other learned
professors of divinity, who could not endure to hear him called
Perkin.   The Lord FitzWater, Sir William Stanley, Sir
Simon Mountford, Sir Robert Ratcliffe, Sir William Daubeny
(as martyrs of state,) confirmed their testimonies with their
blood.   So did the king's serjeant Ferrier, who left the king's
service, and applyed himself to Perkin for which he was executed as a traitor; also Corbet, Sir Quinton Betts, and Gase,
gentlemen of good worth, with 200 more, at least, put to
death in sundry cities and towns, and about London for their
confidence and opinions in this prince.   Richard Grafton
affirmeth the same; in Flanders (saith he,) and most of all
here in England, it was received for an undoubted truth, not
only of the people, but of the nobles, that Perkin was the son
of King Edward the Fourth.   And they all swore and affirmed
this to be true; the learned and famous Mr. Cambden avoweth
there were many wise, grave, and persons of good intelligence,
(who lived in that time and near it,) that affirmed confidently
this Perkin was second son to King Edward."—Buck's Life
of Rich. III., p. 84 and 100.

F.

THE LADY MARGARET'S VOW.

(See p. 195.)

This document is contained in an old register called the
"Thin Red Book," and is preserved in the Library of St.
John's College, Cambridge.

G.

TABLE SHEWING THE DESCENT OF EDWARD PRESENT EARL OF DERBY, K. G., FROM MARGARET COUNTESS OF RICHMOND AND DERBY.

(See page 201.)

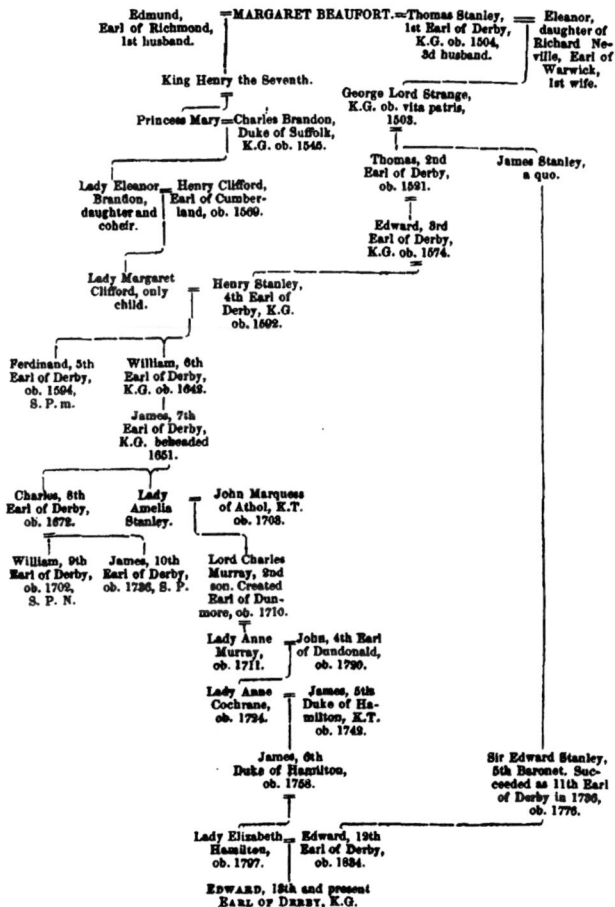

8

H.

(See p. 912)

A most curious document both as regards the description of
dress then in use, and the importance attached to prescribing
due limits, to "the wearing of barbes, over the chin and
under at funerals." The barbe was a kind of chin cloth of fine
linen worn by mourners. No lady under the degree of a
baroness was permitted to wear them over the chin. Knights'
wives were to wear them under their chins, and esquires' wives
and gentlewomen of note wore them beneath their throats.[1]
The Lady Margaret's ordinance prescribed also the size of the
mantle, form of the mourning garment beneath, and fixed the
length of the train. These orders it would seem were framed
by command of King Henry VII., in consequence of the
adoption by mean persons of the costume then exclusively
appropriated to women of quality. A countess was allowed to
have a "trayne before and another behinde, but a baroness no
trayne. The trayne before to be narrow, not exceeding the
breadth of eight inches, and must be trussed up before under
the girdle, or borne upon her left arm."

The King's deference for the opinion of his mother was strikingly marked throughout his reign. At an earlier period of
which, in obedience to his request, she also drew up ordinances
relative to the preparations and etiquette to be observed preparatory to the accouchement of the Queen of England, and the
christening of the royal infants, their progeny. A relic of
antiquity equally curious as the last, composed with great care
and attention, and concluding by an order that the honourable
ladies in attendance on Her Majesty shall, " be made all man-

[1] Vetusta Monumenta, Vol. II. p. 5.

ner of officers, as butlers, stewards, &c. ; the officers they represented being commanded to bring them all needful things unto the greate chambre door, and the women officers to receive it there of them." Amongst sundry other amusing preparations is enjoined " a little cradell of tree, of a yard and a quarter large, and twenty-two inches broad, in a frame set forthe by painters crafte, superbly furnished with clothe of golde, ermyn fur, and crimson velute."

Leland's Collec. Vol. IV. p. 183.
Harl. MSS. 6079.

I.

RELIGIOUS SANCTUARIES.

(See p. 229.)

Until the reign of King Henry the Eighth, all churches and churchyards were sanctuaries ; and protected traitors, thieves, murderers, &c., if within forty days they acknowledged their fault, and submitted themselves to banishment. The most eminent sanctuaries in England were Westminster ; St. Martin's-le-Grand ; Rippon, in Yorkshire ; St. John's, of Beverley, and St. Burien's, in Cornwall.

Paston Letters, Vol. II. p. 79.

K.

EPITAPH INSCRIBED UPON THE TOMB OF MARGARET, COUNT-
ESS OF RICHMOND AND DERBY, INTERRED IN HENRY VII.
CHAPEL, IN WESTMINSTER ABBEY.

(See p. 234.)

MARGARETAE. RICHEMONDIAE. SEPTIMI. HENRICI.
MATRI. OCTAVI. AVIAE. QVAE. STIPENDIA. CONSTITVIT.
TRIB. HOC. COENOBIO. MONACHIS. ET. DOCTOI. GRAM-
MATICES. APUD. WYMBORN. PERQ: ANGLIUM. TOTAM.
DIVINI. VERBI. PRAECONI. DVOB. ITEM. INTERPRAETIB:
LITTERAR: SACRAR: ALTERI. OXONIIS. ALTERI. CANTA-
BRIGIAE. VBI. ET. COLLEGIA. DVO. CHRISTO. ET. IOANNI.
DISCIPVLO. EIVS. STRVXIT. MORITVR. AN. DOMINI. M. D.
IX. III. KAL. IVLII.

CPSIA information can be obtained at www.ICGtesting.com
Printed in the USA
BVOW051546201011

274143BV00014B/43/A